OVERCOMING ADDICTIVE BEHAVIOR

NEIL T. ANDERSON

MIKE QUARLES

Regal

From Gospel Light
Ventura, California, U.S.A.

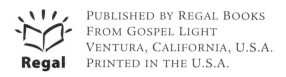

PUBLISHED BY REGAL BOOKS
FROM GOSPEL LIGHT
VENTURA, CALIFORNIA, U.S.A.
PRINTED IN THE U.S.A.

Regal Books is a ministry of Gospel Light, a Christian publisher dedicated to serving the local church. We believe God's vision for Gospel Light is to provide church leaders with biblical, user-friendly materials that will help them evangelize, disciple and minister to children, youth and families.

It is our prayer that this Regal book will help you discover biblical truth for your own life and help you meet the needs of others. May God richly bless you.

For a free catalog of resources from Regal Books/Gospel Light, please call your Christian supplier or contact us at 1-800-4-GOSPEL or www.regalbooks.com.

Cover and interior design by Robert Williams
Edited by Steven Lawson and Stephanie Parrish

Library of Congress Cataloging-in-Publication Data
Anderson, Neil T., 1942–
    Overcoming addictive behavior / Neil T. Anderson and Mike Quarles.
        p. cm.
    Includes bibliographical references.
    ISBN 0-8307-3296-9
    1. Compulsive behavior—Religious aspects—Christianity. 2. Addicts—Religious life. I. Quarles, Mike. II. Title.
    BV4598.7.A53 2003
    248.8'629—dc22   2003015006

4 5 6 7 8 9 10 11 12 13 14 15 16 17 / 11 10 09 08 07 06

Rights for publishing this book in other languages are contracted by Gospel Light Worldwide, the international nonprofit ministry of Gospel Light. Gospel Light Worldwide also provides publishing and technical assistance to international publishers dedicated to producing Sunday School and Vacation Bible School curricula and books in the languages of the world. For additional information, visit www.gospellightworldwide.org; write to Gospel Light Worldwide, P.O. Box 3875, Ventura, CA 93006; or send an e-mail to info@gospellightworldwide.org.

CONTENTS

NOTE TO THE READER

What Is an Addict?

According to *Merriam-Webster's Collegiate Dictionary*, 10th edition, the verb "addict" means "to devote or surrender (oneself) to something habitually or obsessively." An addict is the person who devotes or surrenders himself or herself to that substance. For the sake of our discussion, an addict also is someone who can't seem to break free from habitual sin. Addicts are in the cycle of sin-confess, sin-confess, sin-confess and sin again. Such defeated Christians are stuck in Romans chapter 7: They know what is right, and they want to do what is right; but for some reason they can't seem to do it. This book seeks to explain how they can break out of that cycle and experience their freedom in Christ.

What Is Freedom?

The apostle Paul wrote that "it was for freedom that Christ set us free" (Gal. 5:1). The Christian's state of being is to be alive and free in Christ. God has set His children free, but many are not experiencing that freedom.

The 10th edition of *Merriam-Webster's Collegiate Dictionary* gives this definition for "freedom":

> the quality or state of being free: as **a:** the absence of necessity, coercion, or constraint in choice or action **b:** liberation from slavery or restraint or from the power of another: independence.

This definition addresses two aspects of freedom. The first aspect is freedom of choice. When we have the freedom to choose, it is easy for us to go to an extreme: either license or legalism. If we tend toward license, it is important to remember that choices have consequences and that making the wrong choices can result in bondage. Christians who lean toward legalism should remember that they are free from the external constraints of the Law and from their past, since they are new creations in Christ. "Now the Lord is the Spirit; and where the Spirit of the Lord is, there is liberty" (2 Cor. 3:17). Being free in Christ avoids both license (see Gal. 5:13) and legalism (see Gal. 5:1).

The second aspect of freedom is freedom from slavery. The not-yet Christians may believe that freedom is the absence of any master; but in actuality, they are not without a master, because they are bond servants of sin. Liberated Christians are no longer slaves to sin. They are bond servants of Christ, who set them free to be all that God created them to be. Self-control is a fruit of the Spirit, which is a result of being filled with the Holy Spirit. If we walk by the Spirit, we will not carry out the desires of the flesh (see. Gal. 5:16,22-23)—now, that is freedom!

INTRODUCTION

I was the lead systems engineer on an underwater fire control system, which was a rocket-launched torpedo. Our first production unit had just rolled off the assembly line, and I was laboring night and day to get it operational. A production engineer had been assigned to work with me during the night shift. The kindest way I can put it is that he wasn't much help to me. His wife would call in sick for him at least once a week, so I could never count on him to be there. By the time the night shift came around, I would already be fatigued from working all day. As I labored into the evening, he would sit behind me eating sunflower seeds. It was driving me nuts!

One night out of frustration, I asked him if he ever went to church. He said he wasn't attending any church at the time, but he and his wife had often talked about it. So I invited him to the church I attended, and to my surprise he came. The next Sunday I met him, his wife and their children and helped them find the right Sunday School class.

The following Tuesday morning I got a call from my pastor. "I visited the couple you brought to church last Sunday, and I led them to Christ," he said. I was elated. "Since he works with you," he continued, "I thought it would be helpful for you to know that he is an alcoholic." That revelation put everything else into perspective. That was why he missed work periodically and why he munched on sunflower seeds.

Working with people who struggle with addictive behaviors can be frustrating. It is even more exasperating for those who have to live with them. As difficult as it is for others, it is even more devastating for those who can't seem to overcome the particular behavior.

> Who has woe? Who has sorrow? Who has contentions? Who has complaining? Who has wounds without cause? Who has redness of eyes? Those who linger long over wine, those who go to taste mixed wine (Prov. 23:29-30).

They are living a mental, emotional and physical nightmare. Some keep their ordeal private and expend great effort to hide their addiction. Others make life miserable for everyone and anyone around them.

Why do people with an addictive behavior stay on a destructive course? Why would some keep pouring alcohol into their body, knowing that it is destroying everything that has meaning to them, particularly their family, career and health? Why would others keep sticking needles into their veins, knowing that it is a death warrant? Why would people keep snorting drugs, knowing what it will eventually do to their brain, much less the damage it does to their nasal membranes? Why do so many go back again and again to pornography on the Internet?

Do addicts enjoy being addicted? No, of course they don't, no matter how hard some may try to convince us otherwise. People with an addictive behavior may enjoy the high for a short time, but the next day is horrible. They do not make rational decisions, thus trying to reason with them about a certain destructive behavior has very little impact. People don't make decisions with the intention of destroying themselves—at least not initially.

I can't imagine a teenager saying "When I grow up, I would like to be an alcoholic," "When I am older I want to be grossly overweight due to excessive eating" or "I am going to become a chain smoker so that I will have cancer someday!" Most people addicted to sex, drugs, alcohol, tobacco or food thought at one time, *That will never happen to me. I can stop anytime I want.*

Nobody is born with the mental aspect of addiction to alcohol or drugs, although a newborn baby can have severe physical problems due to his or her mother's addiction to alcohol or drugs. People become addicted by a series of choices that they make in the process of growing older—although, I hesitate to call it "growing up," because addictions severely inhibit maturation. In the same way, nobody is offered at birth a career in engineering, medicine, law or ministry. People achieve those prominent positions by a series of choices and hard work. If they are successful, it is because they assumed responsibility for their own attitudes and actions.

We should, however, be careful about rushing to judgment. If we had been subjected to the same harsh treatment that many of these people had to endure, we would have been tempted to make the same decisions they have made. If we had the same parents, family and neighbors they had, it is very likely that we would be struggling as they are.

Most addicts are products of their past and are very needy. Children growing up in single-parent families are twice as likely as their counterparts to develop serious psychiatric illnesses and addictions later in life, according to a recent study that tracked about 1 million children for a decade—into their mid-20s. Females were three times as likely to become drug addicts if they lived with only one parent; males four times as likely.[1] Given the decline of the nuclear family and the high percentage of broken homes, we are facing a huge problem.

Who are the alcoholics? It may surprise you. One of the biggest myths about alcohol is that the primary abusers are so-called rednecks, the uneducated and the blue-collar workers. Not true! I have gathered the following figures from a variety of sources and rounded off the numbers so that you can have a rough idea who the substance abusers are:

According to Gender
75 percent are men
25 percent are women

According to Occupation
45 percent are professionals and/or management
25 percent are white collar
30 percent are blue collar

According to Education
50 percent attended or graduated from college
37 percent attended or graduated from high school
13 percent fell into other categories

It is easy to see the problem in our drug-infested inner city and miss the plight of the suburbs. In the rash of school shootings, did you notice that these disturbed children were Caucasian and came from middle- to upper-middle-class homes? Our appearance- and performance-oriented culture is inundated with diet and exercise programs, yet the average American continues to grow fatter and get sicker. HIV is one of the most incurable diseases plaguing the world, and it is easily the most preventable. All we have to do is abstain from sex and drugs. Why can't we just say no? Even our government has given up on its Just Say No campaign, which didn't work.

I was reading a newspaper article about a woman who had been commissioned by the state board of education to lecture students on the subject of safe sex. The assumption was that if students only knew the dangers of sexually transmitted diseases, they would behave properly. The lady assigned this awesome responsibility happened to have a weight problem. Consequently, she had devoured books on nutrition, exercise and diet. She probably knew enough to give lectures on those subjects as well, but knowing all that information didn't stop her from having a second piece of pie on the day she was thinking about the formidable task ahead of her. How insightful! She knew from her own experience that telling people what they are doing is wrong does not give them the power to stop doing it. If that approach didn't work for her as an adult, how could she expect it to work for children?

Obviously, laying down the law does not work—it never has and it never will. That is the first reason why most diet and recovery programs don't work. Most are law based. The participants have to stop doing something and start doing something else. Some programs cut that formula in half and make abstinence the goal. Even if the participants manage to stop their particular addictive behavior, the result is dry drunks or addicts who may be more miserable than before. The very thing they had been using to deal with their pain or cope with the problems of life is taken away from them; but they are still products of their past, with incredible needs and stunted growth. They haven't learned to cope with life and deal with their pain in healthy ways.

Secular programs tend to focus on harmful behavior. The participants in the programs assume an identity of failure and struggle to change their behavior. People don't just have sexual addictions, take drugs or eat too much, however; rather, they have life problems. Even some secular programs have recognized their deficiency and attempt to incorporate the family into the recovery process, but that is not enough. The addict and the family are still working the program, and there is not a program in the world that can set them free. The Bible teaches that performance-oriented living, or legalism, "kills, but the Spirit gives life. Now the Lord is the Spirit; and where the Spirit of the Lord is, there is liberty" (2 Cor. 3:6,17).

The good news is that people can be free from their past, become new creations in Christ and have all their critical needs met in Jesus. That is the message of the gospel, made possible by a forgiving and loving God. When this is fully understood and appropriated, people can walk by the Spirit and not carry out the desires of the flesh (see Gal. 5:16). The fruits of the Spirit are love, joy, peace, patience, kindness, goodness, faithfulness, gentleness and self-control. The fruits of the flesh are hatred (mostly of self), depression, fear, anxiety, impatience, unfaithfulness and loss of control.

The purpose of this book is to show how being alive and free in Christ is the answer for overcoming habitual sin and how the truth of God's Word will set us free. I will begin by discussing how addictive behaviors are formed. A simple explanation of why we do what we do, however, can be used as nothing more than an excuse for continuing our self-destructive behaviors. Telling a person why he or she drinks may only result in his or her saying, "You're right—do you want to drink with me?" I have no desire to help anyone just cope with addiction. Freedom from the bondage of sin is the goal, and that will require knowing the truth about our new identity and position in Christ.

Transformation also requires the renewing of our mind. So we will consider the ongoing battle for our mind and learn how we can tear down mental strongholds that have been raised up against the knowledge of God (see 2 Cor. 10:5).

I will address many kinds of addictions, but the theology to overcome each is the same. The good news is we don't have to live in bondage to our sins of the past. None of us can fix our past, but by the grace of God we can all be free of its shackles. Jesus didn't come to give us coping skills; He came to give us life and make us new creations in Him. That is what enables us to live a righteous life, but we can't do it by keeping the law or by submitting to some program. The liberated Christian lives by faith according to what God says is true in the power of the Holy Spirit.

It is my prayer that the Holy Spirit will guide you into all truth and that the truth will set you free to be all that God has called you to be. Before we move on to chapter 1, let's look at an encouraging testimony someone, who shall remain anonymous, sent to my ministry:

> I was raised in what everyone would think was a perfect home. My parents were Christians and pillars of the church. When I reached puberty, like every other boy I was interested in sex. My parents weren't very good at sharing at an intimate level, so most of what I learned about sex was from my friends and a book my parents had in the house. From the book, I learned how to masturbate and before long I became a slave to it. I was in my own private world. On the outside I was this Christian kid, involved with the youth group, a counselor at a Christian camp, and a member of the "perfect family." On the inside I was in complete bondage to pornography and lustful thinking.

I went to a Christian college, where I continued to feed my lustful habits. I knew the stores that sold pornography. I married my beautiful Christian girl-friend, and we were the "perfect couple." But I still had this private world that my wife didn't even know about. My addiction continued to get worse since I was on the road a lot with my job, and I got closer and closer to the edge (adultery). I thought I could dabble with pornography, but never commit the "big one." Of course it finally happened, and then it happened again and again. I knew it was wrong, but I couldn't stop. I would have guilt and remorse, but no true repentance.

Finally, events orchestrated by God led to my wife finding out about my sexual addiction. I confessed to her and God my life of bondage to pornography and sex. I fell to my knees before God and repented of my sin, and for the first time truly felt the love and grace of my heavenly Father.

With the help of your books, I was able to discover my freedom in Christ. Never before have I felt such freedom! I am truly alive in Christ. No more bondage! No more slavery to sin![2]

Notes

1. "Broken Homes Contribute to Substance Abuse," *Arizona Republic*, January 24, 2003, sec. A, p. 11.
2. Anonymous letter written to Neil Anderson at Freedom in Christ Ministries.

WHY DO WE DO IT?

*Sin is not hurtful because it is forbidden, but sin is
forbidden because it is hurtful.*

ARTHUR H. ELFSTRAND

*Some psychological and sociological conditioning occurs in every man's life and
this affects the decisions he makes. But we must resist the modern concept that
all sin can be explained merely on the basis of conditioning.*

FRANCIS A. SCHAEFFER

One of my seminary students walked into my office and slowly
closed the door. "I'm checking out of seminary," he said. His eyes
never left the floor as he stood nervously in front of me, waiting
for my response. Not everybody makes it through seminary, so

this was not totally uncommon. He was a decent student, but he did have a tendency to miss more classes than he should.

"Why are you leaving?" I asked.

The fidgeting became more noticeable before he finally responded, "I guess I'm an alcoholic."

"So why are you dropping out?" I asked. I think he was a little surprised by my response. Most people struggling with addictive behaviors in Christian circles fear the possibility of being found out, and they expect the hammer to fall when they are. That student and I had a long talk that afternoon, and we began to construct a plan for his recovery. Fortunately, he had a good pastor who I knew would work with us to help him break free from his addiction.

One of the more meaningful graduations that I ever attended as a seminary professor came two years later when he walked across that platform and received his diploma—two years sober. I suppose it is a little unusual for a seminary student to be hooked on alcohol, but it is not unusual to find this and other problems in our churches or in Christian ministries.

There are approximately 20 million alcoholics in the United States. It is estimated that 25 percent of these alcoholics are teenagers. Of those who claim to be social drinkers, 1 in 10 is an alcoholic. That ratio is 1 in 3 for those social drinkers who attend a church. Christians are more likely to be secretive about their drinking, which is counterproductive to their Christian walk as well as their recovery in Christ.

What is more common, however, is the problem of sexual addiction. I surveyed the student body of a respected evangelical seminary and found that 60 percent felt guilty because of their sex lives.

With the proliferation of gaming casinos and state-run lotteries, it is estimated that there are more people addicted to gambling than alcohol. In many evangelical churches, it isn't socially acceptable to drink alcohol (at least hard alcohol) or gamble, so we have our own ways of dealing with stress. We eat (too much) and call it fellowship. Casting our anxieties upon the refrigerator will not be healthy in the end (pardon the pun).

Why do people—including believers—choose such destructive behaviors?

PARTYING PROBLEMS AWAY

When I was an engineering student, one night my wife and I had dinner with an Air Force captain and his wife. The captain's wife complained that her cocktail was not strong enough. "It didn't even give me a buzz," she complained. She needed a strong drink to free herself from her inhibitions. She couldn't have fun without dulling her conscience and laying aside her problems and responsibilities. Many people do not particularly care to get drunk, and some manage their consumption very well by setting a limit beforehand. Others don't seem to know when to stop, or they intentionally look for a buzz.

The Peer-Pressure Predicament

Some chemical abusers start and continue their habits in response to peer pressure. I once spoke at a Parents Without Partners meeting, which was on a Friday evening. My message on parenting was sandwiched between the happy hour and the dance. At the meeting, my wife and I struck up a conversation with a single mother who had a cigarette in one hand and a drink in the other. As we talked, the cigarette burned itself out and the ice cubes melted in her drink. This woman told us that on any other occasion she neither smoked nor drank. So why was she doing it here? Peer pressure! It was the social thing to do. In some settings a person would really stand out if he or she didn't do what everybody else was doing.

While smoking no longer holds the same status in most social circles, drinking certainly does. Why do people go to such events and why do they do things they otherwise would not do? Probably because we all have a need to be accepted and to have a sense of belonging.

Many Christians in business find themselves in compromising positions. They battle thoughts such as, *I don't really care to drink, but to make a business deal I'd better go along with the luncheon plans and cocktail party. If I don't go along with what they are doing, they may think I won't play ball with them. This is not the time to make some moral stand. They may take offense if I look down my nose at their drinking habits. It could kill the deal.*

A very successful corporate officer once told me that his unlimited expense card could buy him any vice he wanted, including a "massage." Of course, his company made such vices available discreetly, with no questions asked. Certainly this man and others like him are tempted: *Who would know? The company expects me to take a few perks and write them off as business expenses. I work hard and I deserve some fun. Everyone else does it, don't they?*

> WE ARE MORE VULNERABLE TO TEMPTATION WHEN OUR LEGITIMATE NEEDS ARE NOT BEING MET.

How well we stand against peer pressure and resist the temptation to throw off our inhibitions and party is dependent on how secure we are and how well our basic needs are being met.

These are probably the primary reasons why young people drink, take drugs or compromise sexually. No one wants to be the odd person out. The nerd! The party pooper! Very few young people are secure enough in their identities to be able to stand alone. People are better able to stand against such peer pressure when they have another group that will accept them and provide them with a sense of belonging.

We are more vulnerable to temptation when our legitimate needs are not being met. The question is, Are they going to be met in Christ, who promised to meet all of our needs according to His riches in glory (see Phil. 4:19)? Or are we going to succumb to temptation and turn to the counterfeit attempts to fulfill our needs, as offered in abundance by the world, the flesh and the devil? Paul admonished, "Let our people also learn to engage in good deeds to meet pressing needs, that they may not be unfruitful" (Titus 3:14).

The first puff on a cigarette, the first taste of beer or the first sip of hard liquor is seldom, if ever, a good experience. So why do so many people proceed with an act that their natural tastes and their own body want to reject? Most are driven to fulfill an inner need for acceptance. They want to belong. People tend to compromise their own convictions, and children often ignore the warnings of their parents in order to be accepted by a friend or a group. They do not want to be lonely.

The Rebellion Game

Some people act out of rebellion to authority. They drink alone as a way to prove they are not going to be pushed around or told what to do. They deliberately choose an offensive group to join. These youngsters usually come from dysfunctional homes or legalistic religious settings. Rules without relationship lead to rebellion. Their first taste of a vice is repugnant, too, but they keep rebelling, claiming they don't want love or acceptance from parents or some other authority figure. So goes their thinking, but actually they need to be loved and accepted. They are not going to accept rigid standards or abide by a parent's wishes if love and affirmation are absent.

Initial attempts to overcome a child's rebellious attitude with unconditional love and acceptance will often be rebuffed. He or she may be testing the parent or authority figure to see if he or she is really loved. The child wants to be certain that he or she is not being directed to behave in a particular way just to promote or protect the parent's or authority figure's reputation or ego. *If your own motives are pure, then you have to outlove the child, without compromising what you believe.*

The Great Escape

Work is unbearable. Nobody understands me! My boss is an unreasonable jerk! I didn't have one sale today, and my bills are piling up! Maybe I could get my work done if they would only get off my back! They just laid off another bunch! Am I next? I'll stop off at the club on my way home and have a drink with the boys. It will help me get the pressures of work off my mind and allow me to relax! Just one drink! Well, make it two! How about another for the road?

People drink or use drugs to escape these and other pressures of life. That is what the happy hour is all about. The truth is we all have a lot of pressures in life. However, running away from them or abdicating responsibilities only makes problems worse. Paul wrote:

We also exult in our tribulations, knowing that tribulation brings about perseverance; and perseverance, proven character; and proven character, hope; and hope does not disappoint, because the love of God has been poured out within our hearts through the Holy Spirit who was given to us (Rom. 5:3-5).

Seeking temporary release from our responsibilities with sex, alcohol, drugs and other addictions only increases the pressure. In contrast, hope lies in proven character—not by numbing

> SEEKING TEMPORARY RELEASE
> FROM OUR RESPONSIBILITIES
> WITH SEX, ALCOHOL, DRUGS AND
> OTHER ADDICTIONS ONLY
> INCREASES THE PRESSURE.

our feelings, but by providing a lasting answer. Paul also wrote:

Not that I speak from want; for I have learned to be content in whatever circumstances I am. I know how to get along with humble means, and I also know how to live in prosperity; in any and every circumstance I have learned the secret of being filled and going hungry, both of having abundance and suffering need. I can do all things through Him who strengthens me (Phil. 4:11-13).

The Survivor Mode

We can learn to live by the grace of God in whatever circumstances we find ourselves. Unfortunately, in order to survive, some people choose to believe that their hope lies in trying to alter their circumstances. As a result, they become possessive controllers, and those around them become codependents. Even the slickest manipulators cannot control all the circumstances of life, so they turn to alcohol and other desensitizers to cover their anguish. These are angry, bitter people.

Other people are overcome by their circumstances and feel absolutely helpless. They drown their sorrows in booze, drugs or sex. They have never learned how to cope with life's pressures. Neither the control freak nor the escapist has learned how to grow through the trials and tribulations of life. This is one of the greatest tragedies of addiction: Growth in character and emotional development are arrested.

The New Testament instructs us to cast all of our anxieties onto Christ because He cares for us and He has our best interests at heart (see 1 Pet. 5:7). The drug dealer and the bartender could care less about their clients. To them, the addictions they dole out are just business—the more a patron uses or drinks, the better.

What makes matters worse is that the cure that chemicals and alcohol pretend to offer is only temporary. When the effects wear off, the addict has to go back to the same world with the same responsibilities, but the circumstances only get worse with each successive trip to the dealer or bar.

The Bar

The Saloon is called a bar.
It is more than that by far!
It's a bar to heaven, a door to hell,
Whoever named it, named it well.
A bar to manliness and wealth;
A door to want and broken health.
A bar to honor, pride and fame;
A door to grief, and sin and shame.
A bar to hope, a bar to prayer;
A door to darkness and despair.
A bar to an honored, useful life;
A door to brawling, senseless strife.
A bar to all that's true and brave;

A door to every drunkard's grave.
A bar to joys that home imparts;
A door to tears and aching hearts.
A bar to heaven, a door to hell;
Whoever named it, named it well.[1]

STOPPING THE PAIN

When you have a throbbing toothache, the only thing on your mind is to stop the pain. You do not care about politics, family or world evangelization. You only desire one thing: stopping the pain. This is another reason people turn to chemicals and alcohol.

Many good people have become addicted to prescription medications because the pain they felt was unbearable. Responsible doctors will not prescribe a dosage that would cause a patient to become chemically addicted, yet some patients find other sources. They may have three or more medical professionals call in separate prescriptions, each to a different pharmacy to avoid detection. Some people mix alcohol with their prescriptions. There are many ways to beat the safeguards that society has set in place, including ordering drugs via the Internet.

> WE HAVE TO LEARN TO LIVE WITH A CERTAIN AMOUNT OF PAIN. IT IS A CRITICAL PART OF GROWING UP.

My heart goes out to anyone who is in great pain because of an injury or illness, but pain is not the enemy. Dr. Paul Brand

and Philip Yancey wrote the insightful book *Pain: The Gift Nobody Wants*. They correctly point out that physical pain is a gift from God. If we could not feel pain, we would be shrouded in a hopeless mask of scars. That does not mean we should throw out all painkillers—sometimes they are necessary. The problem arises because we have become a pill-happy society. Even the slightest pain is unacceptable and must be eliminated immediately—at any cost. This kind of thinking could potentially destroy us, as individuals and as a society. We have to learn to live with a certain amount of pain. It is a critical part of growing up.

The physical pains we feel in the body are not always the worst that we will have to endure in life. The emotional pains of failure, rejection and loss of a loved one can be just as devastating. Years ago I counseled a couple whose story illustrates how deep such hurts can cut. The husband was an exasperating man. His job was not working out; neither was his marriage. I have never seen a man so flat on his back, who nonetheless kept spitting at everybody. By his account, his boss, his wife and even his pastor were all messed up, but he was not! Although we seemed to have made a connection, he even stopped calling me.

Several months after the last time I saw him, I received a telephone call late at night. To my surprise, he had just gotten out of jail. I did not even know that he had been arrested. His wife had left him and his family wanted nothing to do with him, so I was the first person he called. He said, "This is the first time that I have been off drugs in 10 years." I was surprised; I did not even know that he was a user. He had been selling enough drugs at work to pay for his hidden habit. He had called me, and I sensed that he was more open than he had ever been before, so I asked, "Knowing that you were losing your wife, your job and your church, why did you continue to use?" He said, "When I was high was the only time that I ever felt good about myself."

UNDERSTANDING THE
REAL PROBLEM

Regardless of why people choose to drink or take drugs, they all hold at least two of the following three things in common: (1) their basic needs are not being met in a legitimate way; (2) they have not learned how to cope with the problems of life; and (3) they cannot seem to resolve their personal or spiritual conflicts in a responsible way.

Becoming addicted to chemicals will not meet anyone's needs; nor will it enable anyone to cope or resolve conflicts. It will only make matters worse. Nobody plans to become an addict, nor does anybody like it when he or she is addicted. Everybody is sure it will never happen to him or her.

GOING DEEPER

1. With what destructive behaviors have you struggled?
2. Have you ever tried to change your behavior to conform to the expectations of certain groups? What has been the result of that choice?
3. What person, group or activity best gives you a sense of belonging? How is this helpful or harmful when facing peer pressure?
4. What temporary remedies do you use to quell the pains you face in life?

Note
1. Author unknown.

THE PATH TO ADDICTION

*Some of the most dreadful mischiefs that afflict mankind
proceed from wine; it is the cause of disease, quarrels, sedition, idleness,
aversion to labor, and every species of domestic disorder.*

FRANCOIS FENELON

*Habit is a cable; we weave a thread of it every day,
and at last we cannot break it.*

HORACE MANN

The affair between King David of Israel and Bathsheba, wife of
Uriah the Hittite, is a sad illustration of the steps to defilement.

David was called a man after God's own heart (see Acts 13:22), but he had one dark blot on his life. First Kings 15:5 summarizes his life:

> David did what was right in the sight of the LORD, and had not turned aside from anything that He command-ed him all the days of his life, except in the case of Uriah the Hittite.

TRACING THE STEPS TO DEFILEMENT

Consider David's steps to moral defilement (see 2 Sam. 11) and those of his son Amnon (see 2 Sam. 13).

Innocent Infatuation

As David and Amnon illustrate, the first step usually begins with natural desires. There is nothing wrong with being attracted to a member of the opposite sex. God made us that way. Such nat-ural drives are intended for our pleasure, and such will be the case as long we do not cross any moral barriers. David saw that Bathsheba "was very beautiful in appearance" (2 Sam. 11:2). Had he left it at that, everything would have been fine. "But each one is tempted when he is carried away and enticed by his own lust. Then when lust has conceived, it gives birth to sin; and when sin is accomplished, it brings forth death" (Jas. 1:14-15).

Mental Obsession

We cross the line to step two when innocent infatuation turns to mental obsession. Amnon developed an obsessive love (actually lust) for his sister Tamar (see 2 Sam. 13:1). "Amnon was so frus-trated because of his sister Tamar that he made himself ill, for she was a virgin, and it seemed hard to Amnon to do anything to her" (v. 2). When we are tempted, God provides a way of escape. For this to work, we have to win the battle for our mind the moment we recognize the temptation, or we will become mentally obsessed and lust will be conceived.

Expressed Lust

Once lust is conceived, it demands expression—thus the third step becomes unavoidable. When someone reaches this step, he or she has already created a scheme to satisfy his or her lusts. Any believer struggling with addictive behavior will lie and cover up his or her actions, and all rationality will disappear. David slept with Bathsheba, and she became pregnant. To cover up his sin, David called for her husband, Uriah, to come home. David hoped that the couple would sleep together and Uriah would think the baby was his. But Uriah refused to take special privileges while his men were in battle. When David's first plan failed, he arranged for Uriah to be put in harm's way, where he was killed. Amnon likewise arranged for his sister to be brought to him under false circumstances, and he raped her. She tried to reason with him, but he would not listen.

> SEXUALLY ADDICTED PEOPLE CRAVE ANOTHER LOOK, BUT WHEN THEY HAVE HAD THEIR FILL, THEY TEAR UP THE PICTURES AND VOW TO NEVER LOOK AGAIN—UNTIL TOMORROW.

Hated Control

The steps to defilement are complete when people who have erred eventually hate that which now controls them. "Then

Amnon hated her [Tamar] with a very great hatred; for the hatred with which he hated her was greater than the love with which he had loved her" (2 Sam. 13:15).

The lust for whiskey is gone when the bottle is empty and the alcoholic throws it against the wall in disgust. Sexually addicted people crave another look, but when they have had their fill, they tear up the pictures and vow to never look again—until tomorrow. The devil changes his role from tempter to accuser. He whispers, "You sick person, when are you ever going to get over this? How can you call yourself a Christian?" The person is on the downward spiral of sin-confess, sin-confess and sin some more.

Spiraling into Addiction

Each person has his or her unique path to addiction, but the cycle that spirals downward is remarkably universal. Please refer to figure 1, which outlines the common addiction cycle for alcoholics.

The Baseline

When people first drink, gamble, use drugs or become involved in a wrongful sexual relationship, they have a mental, emotional and relational baseline. When partying, they are simply looking for a good time and want to join in the celebration. The first drink, puff, snort or sexual titillation brings an immediate chemical reaction. They feel a rush. Alcohol and drugs do not step on the accelerator; rather, they release the brake. When the chemicals take effect, a girl's touch or the payoff from a slot machine causes a euphoric rush. Getting high can be fun for the moment.

Figure 1

THE ADDICTION CYCLE

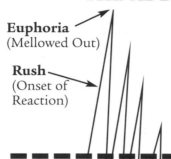

Euphoria
(Mellowed Out)

Rush
(Onset of
Reaction)

Addiction:
1. Habituation
2. Dependency
3. Tolerance
4. Withdrawal

Baseline Experience

Guilt
Fear
Shame

Grandiose, Aggressive
  Behavior

Efforts to Control Fail
  Repeatedly

Tries Geographical Escapes

Family and Friends
  Avoided

Loss of Ordinary
  Willpower

Tremors and Early Morning
  Drinks

Decrease in Ability to Stop
  Drinking

Onset of Lengthy
  Intoxication

Moral Deterioration

Impaired Thinking

Drinking with Inferiors

Unable to Initiate Actions

Obsession with Drinking

All Alibis Exhausted

Occasional Drinking

Increase in Tolerance

Memory Blackouts

Excuses Increase

Surreptitious Drinking

Increased Dependency

Persistent Remorse

Promises Fail

Loss of Interest

Work, Money Troubles

Resentments
  Pile Up

Neglect of Food

Physical
  Deterioration

Irrational Fears

Obsessions

Physical Illness

Complete Defeat

Death or
  Recovery

The baseline experience is different for people who are looking for a temporary reprieve from the pressures of life. Such people can be a bundle of nerves or depressed about their circumstances. They might look for a high to lift their spirits or search for something to calm their nerves. Melancholy people just want to drown their sorrows. Alcohol or drugs will help them mellow out. The quick fix works! Within a matter of minutes they feel better. The same is true for people who want to stop the pain. They cannot wait for that rush to take effect. When it does, they feel better.

Unfortunately, the effect wears off. The morning after is a different story. Addicts wake up feeling just a little bit lower than they did at the baseline experience. Reality sets in, and the head aches. They hardly recognize themselves in the mirror. At work or school, all of the pressures and responsibilities of life come rushing back. There could be twinges of guilt, shame or fear, depending upon the person's conscience. For some people, what they have done is a complete violation of everything they have ever been taught and believed. They now see their euphoric experience as bad and promise that they will never again put themselves in a compromising position.

On the other hand, even on the morning after, party animals will see their euphoric experience as great. They are eager to do it again. It was a lot of fun, something to live for from weekend to weekend, from party to party. The euphoria becomes the center of life. Just thinking about the next experience brings on a rush.

The Cost of the Habit

You feel pain, so you reach for the pills. You feel down, so you do something that will pick you up. You feel stressed out, so you do something that will calm your nerves. It worked before, so it will work again. You have trained yourself to depend on something to pick you up, to stop the pain,

*to soothe your nerves, to make you feel good. You don't believe that you
can have a good time or feel good without it.*

The first step toward addiction is habituation. Occasional
drinking, gambling, sexual titillation or drug use becomes a
habit, a means of emotional support, a crutch to lean on. This
pattern of behavior becomes the means to having a good time or
coping with life. It is a flesh pattern, a defense mechanism.

When the effects wear off, the guilt, fear and shame become
more and more pronounced. With each successive use, addicts
get further and further away from their original baseline experience. When euphoric, they shout, "I am king of the world!" They
are filled with grandiose ideas and often become aggressive. On
the down side, most alcoholics and addicts experience memory
blackouts, and efforts to regain control of their lives fail repeatedly. *How did I get home last night? What happened? I'd better get a grip
on myself—I'm starting to lose control!* Alcoholics feel guilty about
their behavior, so they begin to drink surreptitiously, and they
leave familiar surroundings to go where people don't know
them. They can't live with the shame.

> ## ALCOHOLICS AND ADDICTS WILL NEVER EXPERIENCE THE KIND OF EUPHORIA THEY ONCE DID, NO MATTER HOW MUCH THEY DRINK OR TAKE OR EXPERIENCE.

All they want initially is to reach that elusive high they once
felt and experience the euphoria once more. The problem is it
takes more and more alcohol and a greater fix to reach that orig-

inal high. Users develop their own tolerance levels for their drug of choice (the same happens with people addicted to sex). At first, two beers might have brought on a rush; now it takes a case. Then beer is too slow; a chaser is needed to speed up the process. Marijuana was fine at first; now it takes cocaine. Aspirin used to stop the headache; now it barely has an impact. A kiss was exciting, but that led to petting, and now that isn't enough. Alcoholics and addicts will never experience the kind of euphoria they once did, no matter how much they drink or take or experience. As the lows get lower, so do the potential highs. Before long, all they hope for is to get back to their baseline experience, but even that begins to elude them.

A loss of willpower robs addicts of their ability to live responsible lives at home and eventually at work. The cost to support their habit causes severe financial problems. Many white-collar workers may be able to support their habit for years and carry on their masquerade in public, but their families will suffer tremendous hardship. The poor will steal and become pushers to support their addiction. The morality of both will deteriorate.

Addicts have no sense of worth and no self-respect. They perceive themselves as disgusting. They don't eat well and they don't take care of themselves. Consequently, their physical health becomes a factor.

Withdrawal from social contact is a given for those who are suffering from a chemical addiction. They don't want their weaknesses to be seen or known, and they fear being publicly humiliated or exposed. They become paranoid about people looking at them or talking about them. They have no mental peace. Condemning voices haunt them day and night. *You're disgusting. Why don't you just check out—you're not good for anything. Your family would be better off without you.* The only way to silence those voices is to keep drinking.

EXAMINING YOUR HABITS

Solomon's description of the one who lingers too long over wine ends: "They struck me, but I did not become ill; they beat me, but I did not know it. When shall I awake? I will seek another drink" (Prov. 23:35). To wake up in the morning and desire a drink is a sure sign of alcoholism for some. Others can party on weekends and drink socially for years without that happening. But when the body begins to experience tremors and the only way to stop them is to have a drink, then we know we need help.

How can we know when we are addicted to alcohol? Johns Hopkins University Hospital in Baltimore, Maryland, uses the following test questions to help their patients decide:

	Yes	No
1. Do you lose time from work due to drinking?	___	___
2. Is drinking making your home life unhappy?	___	___
3. Do you drink because you are shy with other people?	___	___
4. Is drinking affecting your reputation?	___	___
5. Have you ever felt remorse after drinking?	___	___
6. Have you gotten into financial difficulties because of drinking?	___	___
7. Do you turn to lower companions and an inferior environment when drinking?	___	___
8. Does drinking make you careless of your family's welfare?	___	___
9. Has your ambition decreased since drinking?	___	___
10. Do you crave a drink at a definite time daily?	___	___
11. Do you want a drink the next morning?	___	___
12. Does drinking cause you to have difficulty in sleeping?	___	___
13. Has your efficiency decreased since drinking?	___	___

14. Is drinking jeopardizing your job or business?   ___   ___
15. Do you drink to escape from worries or trouble?   ___   ___
16. Do you drink alone?   ___   ___
17. Have you ever had a complete loss of memory
    as a result of drinking?   ___   ___
18. Has your physician ever treated you for
    drinking?   ___   ___
19. Do you drink to build up your self-confidence?   ___   ___
20. Have you ever been to a hospital or institution
    on account of drinking?   ___   ___

According to Johns Hopkins University Hospital, if you have answered yes to any one of the questions, this is a definite *warning that you may be an alcoholic*. If you have answered yes to any two, the *chances are that you are an alcoholic*. If you have answered yes to three or more, *you are definitely an alcoholic*.

ADMITTING THE PROBLEM

My first experience with an alcohol recovery program was eye opening. I was sitting with a group of people who were identifying themselves as being a coaddict or co-alcoholic, and codependent. They were in the program to help their friend or another member of their family. Each person had to write out his or her own life story and share it with the group. One couple was there to help their daughter, who was the classic party animal. She could out-drink anybody, which had become a point of pride for her, but now she couldn't stop. It was a painful experience for the mother to share her own personal story, but she got through it. She was more than willing to do whatever it took to help her daughter.

The father had a terrible time sharing his life story. It was short and very superficial. You could tell that he had never been able to share his inner self. The others weren't going to let him get away with it. They began to question him without mercy. I was a little upset. I sat there thinking, *Come on! Give the guy a break. He's here for his daughter. Back off a little!* After tearing down his story, they pursued his present life. "Do you ever drink?" they asked.

"A little I suppose, a beer now and then," he answered.

"How many beers?" they prodded.

"I suppose I occasionally have a few at home," he responded

"How many are a few, and how many nights a week do you have a few?" they relentlessly questioned.

As he struggled to answer, his wife suddenly began to cry. Out came years of frustration and embarrassment, the untold other side of the story that she had only partly shared earlier.

> ## SPEAKING THE TRUTH AND HOLDING YOUR GROUND IN TOUGH LOVE ARE ESSENTIAL FOR GETTING ADDICTS TO SEEK THE HELP THEY NEED.

I'm glad I kept my mouth shut during their inquisition, because he probably would have conned me, but he couldn't fool them. Within 30 minutes they exposed a drinking habit that had existed for years. The first step in recovery is to admit you have a problem and start speaking the truth. As long as people think they can hide their addiction or believe they can live with it, they will probably try to do just that. It used to be a widely held belief that people couldn't be helped until they reached the bottom. Addicts had to wait until they lost their job, health and marriage. Then they would finally admit to the problem and seek the help they so desperately needed, or they would head for skid row and death.

Professional groups now are practicing something called an intervention. This requires some experienced help, because family members have often been too judgmental and condemning or too busy covering up and pretending that all is well. The professional group gathers together all the principal people (including the boss at work) in the alcoholic's or addict's life for a well-orchestrated confrontation. They often rehearse the intervention several times without the alcoholic's knowledge. It has to take place at a time when he or she is sober. Each person in the group then relates what the alcoholic's addiction is doing to him or her personally and to the alcoholic. The alcoholic or addict is then given an opportunity to seek treatment. Speaking the truth and holding your ground in tough love are essential for getting addicts to seek the help they need, since they are on a downward spiral that will eventually destroy them and all that has meaning in life.

Sex addiction is a little different. Sex addicts can hide their addiction for years. You can be the president of the United States and be sexually addicted, but you can't be chemically addicted and maintain that level of responsibility. Drug addicts and alcoholics need chemicals to support their habit, but sex addicts can carry on an affair in their mind. Sexual images and experiences can feed a habit for years. The problem is they can't seem to clean up their mind. Three viewings of pornography can have the same lasting impression on the mind as the actual sexual experience.

ELIMINATING CODEPENDENCY

The downward spiral that all addicts find themselves in is like a tornado that gathers up victims in its path and hurls them out of the way. The primary victims are the other family members.

The spouse is the first affected. When I was pastoring a church, a faithful attendee and worker in the congregation made an appointment to see me. I hardly knew her husband since he seldom went with her to church. I assumed he just wasn't interested in spiritual things. His wife had often requested prayer for his salvation, but she had never shared the family secret. Twenty years of silence were broken that afternoon. She couldn't live that way any longer. His alcoholism had destroyed their family and their marriage. I felt sick that she had waited so long to share her problem.

For 20 years she had been the classic enabler. If he couldn't make it to work because of his drinking, she covered for him. If he passed out drunk on the front lawn, she would somehow get him in the house, clean him up and put him to bed. The children were told to do the same. They had to protect the family name and make sure the chief breadwinner didn't lose his job. Lying and covering up became the means of survival. Family members were threatened if they didn't play along; and even if they did play the game, they still suffered mentally, emotionally and physically. The shame they bore kept them locked in silence.

Enablers have learned to cope and survive by lying and covering up. The fear of retaliation keeps their mouths shut. Their identities and sense of worth are shattered by what is happening at home. They aren't going to lose their last shred of dignity by blowing the whistle. Some people would blame them for breaking up the family, which actually happens in some abuse cases. The biblical mandates to speak the truth in love (see Eph. 4:15) and to walk in the light (see 1 John 1:7) are abandoned for self-preservation. But just the opposite occurs: self-destruction. Enablers are in bondage to their own lies and bitterness.

I asked the lady in my church why she had continued to lie and cover up for her husband. She said, "I was too embarrassed to tell anyone, and I was afraid that he would leave me if I didn't do what I was told."

I said, "As long as you continue to lie and cover up for him, you are enabling him to remain a drunk."

If someone is traveling down a road to destruction, do we want to enable the process? We would not be helping them; we would only be hurting them and hurting ourselves by violating the Word of God. We will never help the addict and the abuser by enabling them to continue in their irresponsible behavior. It will only get worse both for the enabler and for the addict.

> ADDICTS ARE LIKE MISBEHAVING LITTLE CHILDREN WHO ARE SCREAMING FOR ATTENTION: *DOESN'T ANYBODY CARE ENOUGH ABOUT ME TO STOP ME FROM DESTROYING MYSELF?*

Furthermore, enabling undermines the most important relationship we have, which is our relationship with God. All who are involved—the enabler and the addict—are victimized by the father of lies, the prince of darkness.

What should we do when we discover that people we love have an addictive behavior and will not deal with it? Turn them in to their boss, their church and even the police, if a law has been broken. I'm not advocating this because I don't care for addicts, but because I do care for them. They are like misbehaving little children who are screaming for attention: *Doesn't anybody care enough about me to stop me from destroying myself?*

Discipline is a proof of our love, not a violation of it. The fear of being exposed is worse than the actual consequences of being exposed. The consequences of not doing anything about an addiction are worse than the consequences of taking a stand for everybody's sake.

Talk to your addicted loved ones first. Tell them you love them, which is why you aren't going to tolerate their substance abuse any longer. Let them know that you will do whatever it takes for them to be free of their addiction. Most will probably deny that they have a problem. If this happens, let them know that you will no longer lie or cover up for them and that you are going to seek help for yourself. Then, with their knowledge, make an appointment with your pastor. You need moral support and spiritual advice. Find a Christian-based ministry that supports spouses and children of alcoholics. Seek professional help to set up an intervention. You must do something constructive for yourself.

On the other hand, every loving Christian is codependent in a good sense. We are commanded to love one another. That means we are subject to one another's needs. That is not wrong—that is Christlike. However, to be like Christ, that love must be tough when the situation calls for it. It becomes wrong when other people dictate how and when we are to love them. They are controlling us with their sickness. We are not subject to one another's wants or addictions. The moment we are, their bondage becomes our bondage. The Spirit of God enables us to have self-control. That same Holy Spirit will lead us into all truth—the truth that will set us free. Nobody on planet Earth can keep us from being the people that God wants us to be. Both the addict and the coaddict need to find their freedom in Christ, and that is what the rest of this book is all about.

GOING DEEPER

1. Is there any area in your life in which you have crossed the line, going from innocent infatuation to mental obsession?
2. Have you ever lied and schemed to cover up any behavior that you didn't want others to know about? Explain what happened.
3. Review the 20 questions listed in this chapter. Do you know anyone who would fail the test?
4. How do addictive behaviors (yours or someone else's) affect members of your family?

THE ULTIMATE CAUSE OF ALL ADDICTIONS

*Of man's first disobedience, and the fruit of that forbidden tree,
whose mortal taste brought death into the world, and all our woe, with loss
of Eden, till one greater Man restore us, and regain the
blissful seat, sing, Heavenly Muse.*

JOHN MILTON

*Sin has always been an ugly word, but it has been made so in a
new sense over the last half-century. It has been made not only ugly
but passé. People are no longer sinful, they are only immature or
underprivileged or frightened, or particularly, sick.*

PHYLLIS MCGINLEY

Jonathan Melvoin was a backup keyboard player for the rock group Smashing Pumpkins. On the night of July 11, 1996, he died of a drug overdose. The drug that killed him is a genus of heroin, which is known on the streets as red rum—that is "murder" spelled backward.

When the news of Melvoin's death hit the media, it caused a shocking reaction among other drug users on Manhattan's Lower East Side. The demand for red rum skyrocketed! "When people die from something, or nearly die," explained one police official, "all of a sudden, there's a rush to get it because it must be more powerful and deliver a better high."[1]

That is insanity. Such irrationality, however, is not that uncommon for people who live in bondage to sin. How did we ever get this way?

BACKING UP TO THE BEGINNING

To understand the condition and mind-set of our current culture, we need to look at the bigger picture. Let's start with a look at the original creation of Earth and humankind:

> God said, "Let Us make man in Our image, according to Our likeness; and let them rule over the fish of the sea and over the birds of the sky and over the cattle and over all the earth" (Gen. 1:26).

> Then the LORD God formed man of dust from the ground, and breathed into his nostrils the breath of life; and man became a living being (Gen. 2:7).

> The LORD God said, "It is not good for the man to be alone; I will make him a helper suitable for him" (Gen. 2:18).

> The man and his wife were both naked and were not
> ashamed (Gen. 2:25).

God created humankind in His own image. He breathed life into
a hunk of clay, and instantly Adam was spiritually and physically alive. But something was missing. It was not good for Adam to
be alone, and no animal form of life could fulfill this particular
need. So God created a helpmate that was suitable for Adam.
They were naked and unashamed. No part of their body was
considered dirty—they could even have an intimate sexual relationship with each other in the presence of God. There was no
sin, nothing to hide and no reason to cover up.

Adam and Eve were supposed to rule over the rest of God's
creation. God placed them in the "Garden of Eden to work it and
take care of it" (Gen. 2:15, *NIV*). By being fruitful and multiply-
ing they could fill the earth. They were afforded a tremendous
amount of freedom as long as they remained in a dependent
relationship with God. They had a perfect life and could have
lived forever in His presence. They had a divine purpose for
being alive. They had no need to search for significance or strive
for acceptance. They were accepted, significant and secure in the
presence of God. They also had a sense of belonging to God and
to each other. God had provided for all of their needs.

The Fall of Adam and Eve
The ability to think and make choices was inherent in creation,
because Adam and Eve were created in the image of God.
However, there was an evil presence in the universe. The Lord
wanted to change that. Therefore, He commanded Adam and Eve
not to eat from the tree of the knowledge of good and evil (see
Gen. 2:17). They would die if they did. Yet Satan was not going to
sit by silently and watch God's plan to rid the universe of evil go
uncontested. So he questioned and twisted God's words, thus

tempting Eve (see Gen. 3:1-6). He employed the same three channels of temptation that exist today: "the lust of the flesh and the lust of the eyes and the boastful pride of life" (1 John 2:16). Deceived by the craftiness of Satan, Adam and Eve made a choice and thus declared their own independence. They died!

> THE EFFECTS OF ADAM AND EVE'S SIN WERE IMMEDIATE. ALL THE PERSONAL ATTRIBUTES THAT HAD BEEN INHERENT IN CREATION— SPIRITUAL LIFE, IDENTITY, ACCEPTANCE, SECURITY AND SIGNIFICANCE—WERE GONE.

On the day of their first sin, Adam and Eve did not die physically, they died spiritually—although physical death would eventually come, also as a consequence of sin (see Rom. 5:12). The effects of their sin were immediate. All the personal attributes that had been inherent in creation—spiritual life, identity, acceptance, security and significance—were gone, and each became a glaring need. Adam's self-perception became one of shame and guilt. He covered his nakedness and hid from God. But the Lord immediately took the initiative by confronting Adam, wanting to know where he was.

> He [Adam] answered, "I heard you in the garden, and I was afraid because I was naked; so I hid." And he said, "Who told you that you were naked? Have you eaten from the

tree that I commanded you not to eat from?" The man said, "The woman you put here with me—she gave me some fruit from the tree, and I ate it" (Gen. 3:10-12, *NIV*).

The Lord knew the answers to the questions, so why did He ask? He was seeking accountability. He wanted Adam to own up to what he had done. Adam responded by blaming Eve and suggesting that maybe God had something to do with his downfall: "After all, God, You created this woman and gave her to me." Blaming others for our own mistakes has been a consistent pattern of fallen human nature ever since. If we are going to recover in Christ, we must break through our own denial and defenses.

The Hope of the Gospel

The fall of Adam and Eve is the only plausible explanation for the degradation of humanity, for which the gospel offers the only hope. When Adam and Eve lost their relationship with God, they were immediately overcome with guilt and shame. The same thing happens to any Christian who struggles with addictive behaviors. Notice the first emotion expressed by Adam after he sinned: "I was afraid because I was naked; so I hid." The fear of being exposed has driven many of us from the light that reveals our sin. Without God's unconditional love and acceptance, we will run from the light or try to discredit the source of the light, as the Pharisees did with Jesus. Satan raises up thoughts against the knowledge of God (see 2 Cor. 10:5), and a deceived humanity mocks His very existence. Unable to live up to God's eternal standards of morality, the fallen must deal with their fear, guilt and shame; and they do it by hiding from God or by attacking Him.

Every descendant of Adam and Eve is born into this world physically alive but spiritually dead (see Eph. 2:1). We are helpless to do anything about it and hopeless without God. No person living independently of God can live a holy life; in fact, most fear their inadequacies will be exposed.

> Everyone who does evil hates the light, and will not come into the light for fear that his deeds will be exposed. But whoever lives by the truth comes into the light, so that it may be seen plainly that what he has done has been done through God (John 3:20-21, *NIV*).

EXPOSING THE TRUTH

Many addicts have told me that they want to be free of whatever bondage besets them. Simply put, they are tired of living a lie. They see that having feelings of guilt and shame on the inside while giving the appearance of having it all together on the outside is no way to live. What they need to understand is that such shame-based living is the consequence of failing to embrace the hope of the gospel and rejecting the grace of God.

The Value of Intervention

In order for addicts to take the first step toward recovery, they must face the truth. Sometimes they will do this on their own. More often they need help, which can come through some type of intervention. The more evident their addictive behavior is to others, the more likely they are to acknowledge their sin. As long as they think they can hide their actions, they probably will try to do so—even when they know that hiding hurts them. Adam hid, but God did not let him get away with it. That was the world's first intervention.

Exposing hypocrisy in the presence of the very people the addict is trying to deceive is tough to do, but it is very effective. When done right, the result is the elimination of the disconnect between inner conviction and outward behavior which is a constant struggle for the Christian who has addictive behaviors. Once exposed, the game is over—which often brings relief to the sinner. The guilt and pain of living a lie can be more devastating than the shame of being exposed.

Of course, intervention followed by confession is just the initial step. The game was over in a hurry for Adam and Eve, but they still had problems.

I used to require my seminary students to attend an Alcoholics Anonymous (AA) meeting and give a report to our class. They were disappointed with the smoking and the foul language at the meetings, but almost every student said in effect, "I wish I could get the people in my church to be as honest as those people were!" Most people attending AA meetings have already been exposed. They no longer have anything to hide. They have found a place that accepts them for who they are, warts and all.

The Importance of Honesty

Some people attend AA meetings that are closed to visitors, and they put on a façade when outside the group. They are still trying to protect their reputations, so they remain anonymous, or at least they try to. Such public denial was tragically played out on the national stage when during his term in office, President Bill Clinton refused to admit to his sexual addiction. Everybody knew what his problem was and still he chose to lie. He could have said, "My fellow Americans, I have had a sexual addiction for many years. It has caused my family and me much pain. I am going to seek some help for my problem, and I would appreciate your prayers. I believe I can continue to be the president you elected and hoped for, and now maybe even a better one." If he had said this publicly, his ratings would have gone even higher, and he would have done a huge service to those who struggle with the same addiction.

Many Christians fear being exposed. They are not necessarily struggling with drugs or alcohol, but many have a lot of problems that they do not want others, especially people at church, to know about. Their marriage could be in trouble or their children could be rebelling, but they will not seek help as long as they think others are not aware of their predicament. However, they will seek assistance when their spouse walks out or when their child is expelled from school, jailed or runs away. Congregations stop bearing fruit when the members refuse to walk in the light and speak the truth in love. Such people rob themselves and their families of the help they need. Too often the cry for relief only comes after exposure, when the damage has already been done.

There still can be help and hope after a point of crisis, and we must never forget that. The church is supposed to be a redeeming community, in which every member is on one rung of the recovery ladder, reaching down to the person on the rung below and helping them rise above their circumstances and addictions. This cannot happen unless there is honesty—about ourselves and with each other.

SECRET SIN ON EARTH IS OPEN SCANDAL IN HEAVEN.

The Patience of God

The Lord won't let us live in hypocrisy for too long. "For nothing is hidden, except to be revealed; nor has anything been secret, but that it should come to light" (Mark 4:22). Secret sin on Earth is open scandal in heaven. The Bible reads, "If we walk in the light as He Himself is in the light, we have fellowship with one another, and the blood of Jesus His Son cleanses us from all sin" (1 John 1:7). Walking in the light is not moral perfection. The next verse underscores the point: "If we say that we have no sin, we are deceiving ourselves, and the truth is not in us" (1 John 1:8).

Walking in the light is a continuous form of confession. It is living in conscious moral agreement with God and in honest relationships with others. Paul admonishes us to lay "aside false-hood, speak truth, each one of you, with his neighbor, for we are members of one another" (Eph. 4:25).

The Lord loves us too much to allow us to walk in darkness and live a lie. He knows it will eventually destroy us. He will give us a lot of slack to come to this conclusion ourselves, but eventually He will expose us for our own good and for the good of others who are being negatively affected by our secret sin. Protecting our pride destroys our walk with God, because "God is opposed to the proud, but gives grace to the humble" (Jas. 4:6).

Someone once asked me, "How are Christians supposed to act?" Christianity is not an act; it is a real thing. We cannot be right with God and not be real. If necessary, God will arrange the events of our lives so that we will have to be real in order to be right with Him. To live a lie is to play right into the hands of the devil, who is the father of lies and the prince of darkness. Truth is not the enemy; it is always a liberating friend. No matter how painful it is initially to face the truth, the consequences will always be better than the consequences of living a lie. "Humble yourselves, therefore, under the mighty hand of God, that He may exalt you at the proper time" (1 Pet. 5:6).

The Hypocrisy Game

We can play the hypocrisy game for a season, but eventually it will take its toll on us personally. The effects of drugs will show within a couple of years. Alcohol can be covered up for a longer period of time. Sexual addictions can remain a private nightmare much longer.

Some years ago I was surprised to discover how many chemically addicted people are also involved in some form of sexual bondage. The percentage is very high. These people will seek treatment for their chemical addiction but probably will not seek counseling for their struggle with lust, pornography or homosexuality. Like any other addiction, they need help long before they are caught. Many chemically dependent people achieve a degree of sobriety in a recovery program, but still they remain in sexual bondage.

OVERCOMING A FALLEN WORLD

After Adam and Eve's initial sin, their understanding was darkened because they were separated from the life of God (see Eph. 4:18). Trying to hide from God revealed that Adam had lost a true understanding of who God is. What exactly Adam was thinking, I am not sure. How can anyone hide from an omnipresent God? The Lord did not create humankind to live independently of Him, and it is most evident in the inability of a person who does not follow God to understand His ways.

The man without the Spirit does not accept the things that come from the Spirit of God, for they are foolishness to him, and he cannot understand them, because they are spiritually discerned (1 Cor. 2:14, *NIV*).

What a dilemma! Satan had usurped the role of God's people and thus became the rebel holder of earthly authority. Satan even tempted Jesus by showing and offering Him the kingdoms of the world if He would bow down and worship him. "I will give you all their authority and splendor, for it has been given to me, and I can give it to anyone I want to" (Luke 4:6, *NIV*). Jesus never corrected Satan's claim over the kingdoms of this world, and He even referred to Satan as the "ruler" (prince) of the world (John 12:31; 14:30; 16:11). Paul called him "the prince of the power of the air, . . . the spirit that is now working in the sons of disobedience" (Eph. 2:2). As a result of his rule, "the whole world is under the control of the evil one" (1 John 5:19, *NIV*).

God's Strategy to Rescue Humankind

God's plan of redemption was under way immediately. The Lord cursed the snake and foretold the downfall of Satan:

> Cursed are you above all the livestock and all the wild animals! You will crawl on your belly and you will eat dust all the days of your life. And I will put enmity between you and the woman, and between your offspring and hers; he will crush your head, and you will strike his heel (Gen. 3:14-15, *NIV*).

At the Cross, "he" (an individual from the woman's seed, namely Christ) will deal a deathblow to Satan's head, while "you" (Satan) will strike Christ's heel. The Latin rendering of the Hebrew root word for strike (*shuph*) suggests that it carries the idea of lying in wait, suggesting a prolonged conflict with the element of expectancy. This cosmic battle is the backdrop for the drama that unfolds in Scripture and continues into our present day. There will be enmity between the spiritual descendants of Satan and those who are in the family of God. We are either children of God (see John 1:12) or sons of disobedience in whom the evil one is now working (see Eph. 2:2). We are either in the domain of darkness or the kingdom of His beloved Son (see Col. 1:13).

The Old Testament ends on a sour note. The Lord's Chosen People are in political bondage to Rome and in spiritual bondage to an apostate Sanhedrin. The glory has departed from the nation of Israel, but the seed of Abraham is about to make His entrance.

> The Word became flesh and made his dwelling among us. We have seen his glory, the glory of the One and Only, who came from the Father, full of grace and truth (John 1:14, *NIV*).

The blessing of Abraham was about to be extended to all the nations of the world.

An Understanding of Human Nature
Throughout the Old Testament nothing happened that changed the basic nature of fallen humanity. "The intent of man's heart is evil from his youth" (Gen. 8:21). Jeremiah said, "The heart is deceitful above all things and beyond cure" (Jer. 17:9, *NIV*). The Law had done nothing to change this.

> For if a law had been given that could impart life, then righteousness would certainly have come by the law. But the Scripture declares that the whole world is a prisoner of sin (Gal. 3:21-22, *NIV*).

Telling people that what they are doing is wrong does not give them the power to stop doing it. The Law is powerless to give life.

Even more discouraging is the statement by Paul that "the sinful passions aroused by the law were at work in our bodies" (Rom. 7:5, *NIV*). The Law actually has the capacity to stimulate the desire to do what it is trying to prohibit. If anyone does not think that is true, they should try telling their children that they can go a certain place but cannot go to another place. The moment a parent says that, where do the children want to go? They want to go to the forbidden place. They probably did not even want to go there until the parent said they could not. The forbidden fruit always appears to be more desirable.

> # THE FORBIDDEN FRUIT ALWAYS APPEARS TO BE MORE DESIRABLE.

Laying down the law will not resolve the sinful passions. The core problem is the basic nature of humankind, not individual acts or behavior patterns.

The Condition of the Heart

The Pharisees were the moral perfectionists (legalists) of the day. Jesus said, "For I tell you that unless your righteousness surpasses that of the Pharisees and the teachers of the law, you will certainly not enter the kingdom of heaven" (Matt. 5:20, *NIV*). His Sermon on the Mount confronted the issue of genuine righteousness, which is determined by the condition of the heart. Here is one excerpt from that famous teaching: "You have heard that it was said, 'Do not commit adultery.' But I tell you that anyone who looks at a woman lustfully has already committed adultery with her in his heart" (Matt. 5:27-28, *NIV*). The person in this illustration did not physically commit adultery; the looking, however, gave evidence that adultery had already been committed in his heart.

Jesus continued His teaching: "If your right eye causes you to sin, gouge it out. . . . And if your right hand causes you to sin, cut it off and throw it away" (vv. 29-30, *NIV*). Does your eye or hand cause you to sin? I do not think so. If we kept cutting off body parts to keep from sinning, we would end up being nothing more than bloodied torsos rolling down the aisles of our churches. Some see this passage as an admonition to take whatever drastic means it takes to stop sinning, thus emphasizing the hideousness of sin: It would be better to be dismembered than to spend eternity apart from Christ. But I do not think that is the point Jesus is trying to make. Physical acts such as taking cold showers to put out the fires of passion or walking blindfolded on a sunbathers' beach may bring temporary relief, but they do not deal with the condition of the heart. Such behavior might be necessary if the only option we had was to live under the Law.

Trying to live a righteous life externally when we are not righteous internally will only result in being "whitewashed tombs, which look beautiful on the outside but on the inside are full of dead men's bones and everything unclean" (Matt. 23:27, *NIV*). It is not what goes into a man that defiles him; it is what comes out.

> For from within, out of men's hearts, come evil thoughts, sexual immorality, theft, murder, adultery, greed, malice, deceit, lewdness, envy, slander, arrogance and folly. All these evils come from inside and make a man "unclean" (Mark 7:21-23, *NIV*).

Paul wrote:

> For as many as are of the works of the Law are under a curse; for it is written, "Cursed is everyone who does not abide by all things written in the book of the Law, to perform them." Now that no one is justified by the Law before God is evident; for, "The righteous man shall live by faith." However, the Law is not of faith; on the contrary, "He who practices them shall live by them." Christ redeemed us

from the curse of the Law, having become a curse for us—
for it is written, "Cursed is everyone who hangs on a tree"—
in order that in Christ Jesus the blessing of Abraham
might come to the Gentiles, so that we might receive the
promise of the Spirit through faith (Gal. 3:10-14).

LOOKING FOR LASTING ANSWERS

Not understanding the passage in Galatians or the full impact of
the gospel, we fall back under the Law. We operate according to
certain regulations or principles that call for us to respond in obedience. The catch phrases are "Just say no" and "Work the program—the program works." We commit ourselves to a program or
institution and try to follow the advice of those in charge. We vol-
untarily agree to be accountable to a sponsor or counselor who is
committed to helping us. With the help of these external constraints and the support of others, some people manage to attain
a degree of sobriety by sheer willpower. Remove those external

> TRYING TO LIVE UNDER
> THE LAW OR TO LIVE UP TO
> THE EXPECTATIONS OF OTHERS
> WILL FAIL IN THE END.

constraints and the help of others, and most people would fall
back to their old habits. Why? They return to their habit because
there was no true change in their basic nature. Trying to live under
the Law or to live up to the expectations of others will fail in the
end. The Law is a taskmaster, a tutor that was intended by God to
lead us to Christ (see Gal. 3:24), which is where we turn next.

GOING DEEPER

1. Why did Adam and Eve die spiritually? What does this mean for us today?
2. Why is it important to be honest with yourself about your life?
3. How does hypocrisy affect your ability to overcome addictions?
4. According to Mark 4:22, what does God do with things that are hidden?
5. What is God's plan of redemption?

Note

1. Craig Larson, *Choice Contemporary Stories and Illustrations* (Grand Rapids, MI: Baker Books, 1998), p. 72.

THE GOOD NEWS

*The measure of God's anger against sin is the measure of the love that is
prepared to forgive the sinner and to love him in spite of his sin.*

DAVID MARTYN LLOYD-JONES

*That God is more near, more real and mighty, more full of love, and more
ready to help every one of us than any one of us realizes, is the underlying message of the Gospels.*

DAVID S. CAIRNS

I was invited to speak at a rescue mission. The audience was a
group of men who were fresh off the streets. Each one had made
a commitment to Christ and was now being discipled. As I
walked into the meeting room, all of the men stood up and
applauded. I looked around to see if Billy Graham had followed

me in. Why were they clapping? I was relieved to learn that they were not cheering for me; rather, they were lauding my message. Although I did not know it at the time, they had been watching a video series I had recorded some years earlier.

The message on the videocassettes was "You are not a derelict, you are not a bum, you are not a drunkard, you are not a pervert, you are not an alcoholic, you are not a drug addict, and you are not a pimp. You are a child of God." The message got through to these men. Knowing that wonderful truth and all that it implies provided the only real answer and lasting hope they needed to overcome the bondage in which they had lived.

> The reason the Son of God appeared was to destroy the devil's work. No one who is born of God will continue to sin, because God's seed remains in him (1 John 3:8-9, *NIV*).

These two verses express what must happen in order for us to live righteous lives in Christ: First, our basic nature has to change. Second, we need to have a means by which we can overcome the evil one, the ruler of this world. We were by nature "children of wrath" (Eph. 2:3). We were formerly shrouded in darkness, but in Christ we are able to walk as "children of light" (Eph. 5:8). Only God can change who we are, but it is our responsibility to believe the truth that will set us free and assume our responsibility to live in a righteous manner.

Paul taught that we were born dead in our trespasses and sins (see Eph. 2:1). That does not mean that we were stillborn. As I have already pointed out, it means that we were born physically alive but spiritually dead, separated from God. The life that Jesus came to give each of us was the same life that Adam and Eve lost when they sinned.

Jesus said, "I came that they might have life, and might have it abundantly" (John 10:10). There was a time when I thought that this verse meant that Jesus came to improve the quality of our *physical* lives on Earth. How wrong I was. Jesus was talking about *spiritual* life and *eternal* life, both of which can only be found in Him. Spiritual life happens when our soul is in union with God. We are alive in Christ. Jesus did not end His point in John 10:10. He also said, "I am the resurrection and the life; he who believes in Me shall live [spiritually] even if he dies [physically]" (John 11:25). In other words, born-again believers are alive in Christ, and our spirit will live on, even after our body dies.

CONSIDERING THE ENTIRE GOSPEL

Many Christians have only a partial understanding of what the gospel declares. They believe that Jesus is the Messiah who came to die for their sins, and they realize that if they believe in Him, they will go to heaven when they die.

What's wrong with that?

First, this partial picture could convey the impression that eternal life is something we get when we die, which is not true.

> ETERNAL LIFE IS NOT SOME-
> THING WE GET WHEN WE DIE.
> EVERY CHILD OF GOD IS ALIVE
> IN CHRIST *RIGHT NOW.*

Read 1 John 5:12 (*NIV*): "He who has the Son has life; he who does not have the Son of God does not have life." Every child of God is alive in Christ *right now.*

For he has rescued us from the dominion of darkness
and brought us into the kingdom of the Son he loves, in
whom we have redemption, the forgiveness of sins (Col.
1:13-14, *NIV*).

Second, the common understanding of the gospel includes
Christ being crucified for our sins, but it often downplays or
overlooks His resurrection—yet that is what resulted in new life
for believers. If we wanted to save a dead person, what would we
do? Give him life? If that was the only thing we did, the person
would die again. To save the dead person, we would have to do
more. For starters, we would have to cure the disease that caused
him to die. This is what Paul alluded to when he wrote, "The
wages of sin is death" (Rom. 6:23).

Yes, Jesus went to the Cross and died for our sins. Is that the
whole gospel? Absolutely not! He was resurrected so that we may
have new life in Him. Now let's finish Romans 6:23: "But the free
gift of God is eternal life in Christ Jesus our Lord." The fact that
we are alive "in Christ" is the necessary truth that we all need to
appropriate—it is our only hope. This truth is summarized in
one verse: "Christ in you, the hope of glory" (Col. 1:27). Our new
lives and position in Christ are what guarantee victory over sin
(we will look at that in the next two chapters).

Third, the fact that Jesus came to undo the works of Satan is
what makes the gospel complete. When I travel in the Third
World, people become very interested when they hear this part of
the gospel. So many of them have been trying to appease various
deities or fend off evil spirits by sacrificing anything from veg-
etables to human beings. They consult their shamans and witch
doctors, who try to manipulate the spiritual world. When I tell
people in these countries that Christ disarmed the gods they
have been serving, they celebrate. In Christ, they have authority
over all other deities. That truth is just as much a part of the

gospel as the fact that our sins have been forgiven. It is also something we need to know if we are going to win the battle for our mind (a subject on which I will elaborate later in this book).

DISCOVERING CONFIDENCE IN CHRIST

Because we are alive in Christ, we have the Spirit of God within us. We have to learn how to live our lives in total dependence upon God. Before we came to Christ, we depended upon parents, the government, doctors and counselors. We turned to chemicals and we relied upon ourselves. After salvation, we can still choose to depend upon these things, but we need to realize that every temptation is an attempt by Satan to get us to live our lives independently of God.

The deceiver is so subtle. He tempts us to put our confidence in programs, strategies and other people. He even convinces us that we can handle life on our own. However, his true aim is to divert our confidence away from God. Paul wrote:

> Not that we are adequate in ourselves to consider any-thing as coming from ourselves, but our adequacy is from God, who also made us adequate as servants of a new covenant, not of the letter [of the Law], but of the Spirit; for the letter kills, but the Spirit gives life (2 Cor. 3:5-6).

Paul had been self-confident under the Law, but Christ intervened. Only after being struck down on the Damascus road was the apostle able to say, "We are the true circumcision, who worship in the Spirit of God and glory in Christ Jesus and put no confidence in the flesh" (Phil. 3:3). Apart from Christ we can do *nothing* to change the basic nature of who we are, neither can we bear fruit that will last for eternity (see John 15:5).

Because we are alive in Christ, we have the assurance that He will meet all of our needs (see Phil. 4:19). In the long run, any attempt to get out of bondage—to alcohol, drugs, gambling or sex—without the essential needs of our lives being met will prove counterproductive. In my book *Who I Am in Christ*, I try to show how Christ meets the most critical needs in our lives, which are what I call the "being" needs: life, identity, acceptance, security and significance. Here are the major points and the corresponding Scriptures. Please read the points out loud.

IN CHRIST

I Am Accepted

John 1:12	I am God's child.
John 15:15	I am Christ's friend.
Rom. 5:1	I have been justified.
1 Cor. 6:17	I am united with the Lord, and I am one spirit with Him.
1 Cor. 6:19-20	I have been bought with a price. I belong to God.
1 Cor. 12:27	I am a member of Christ's Body.
Eph. 1:1	I am a saint.
Eph. 1:5	I have been adopted as God's child.
Eph. 2:18	I have direct access to God through the Holy Spirit.
Col. 1:14	I have been redeemed and forgiven of all my sins.
Col. 2:10	I am complete in Christ.

I Am Secure

Rom. 8:1-2	I am free from condemnation.
Rom. 8:28	I am assured that all things work together for good.
Rom. 8:31-34	I am free from any condemning charges against me.

Rom. 8:35-39 I cannot be separated from the love of God.

2 Cor. 1:21-22 I have been established, anointed and sealed by God.

Phil. 1:6   I am confident that the good work that God has begun in me will be perfected.

Phil. 3:20   I am a citizen of heaven.

Col. 3:3   I am hidden with Christ in God.

2 Tim. 1:7   I have not been given a spirit of fear but of power, love and a sound mind.

Heb. 4:16   I can find grace and mercy to help in time of need.

1 John 5:18 I am born of God and the evil one cannot touch me.

I Am Significant

Matt. 5:13-14 I am the salt and light of the earth.

John 15:1,5 I am a branch of the true vine, a channel of His life.

John 15:16   I have been chosen and appointed to bear fruit.

Acts 1:8   I am a personal witness of Christ.

1 Cor. 3:16 I am God's temple.

2 Cor. 5:17-21 I am a minister of reconciliation for God.

2 Cor. 6:1   I am God's coworker (see 1 Cor. 3:9).

Eph. 2:6   I am seated with Christ in the heavenly realm.

Eph. 2:10   I am God's workmanship.

Eph. 3:12   I may approach God with freedom and confidence.

Phil. 4:13   I can do all things through Christ who strengthens me.

Some people might be tempted to think, *If I believed all of this about myself, I would be prideful.* Not true! To the contrary, if we do not believe every word, we are defeated. These clear statements from Scripture are not true because of what we have done. They are true because of what Christ has done for us, and the only way we can appropriate that truth is by faith. We all share in His rich inheritance and have the power to live victoriously in Christ. Our problem is that we just do not fully grasp this reality. That is why Paul wrote:

> I pray also that the eyes of your heart may be enlightened in order that you may know the hope to which he has called you, the riches of his glorious inheritance in the saints, and his incomparably great power for us who believe (Eph. 1:18-19, *NIV*).

IDENTIFYING OURSELVES AS CHILDREN OF GOD

The lay leader of a recovery ministry in a church where I once spoke told me, "I came to this conference with a gun in my mouth. If I hadn't found my freedom in Christ, I would have pulled the trigger." This dear man had been sober for several years, but he was not experiencing his freedom. Being in a leadership position made it even more difficult for him to admit that he still had problems. He told me, "I had no idea who I was as a child of God!"

Likewise, most people who struggle to get out of bondage to addiction have no understanding or assurance of who they are in Christ and what it means to be a child of God. This is a common denominator with every person I have ever had the privilege of helping, particularly those who were in bondage to sex, alcohol or drugs. Before they seek help, their self-perception is extremely negative. The accuser of the brethren is having a field day. Those who are in treatment identify themselves as alcoholics, addicts or coaddicts. Thus they succumb to conventional wisdom, which teaches that they cannot be helped nor will anyone be able to help them, unless they admit that they have a problem. Of course, addicts must acknowledge that they have a problem, but Christians with such a problem should not be identified as alcoholics or addicts, nor should they constantly repeat self-deflating statements about who they are. These people are children of God who are struggling to overcome their bondage. They are not sinners in the hands of an angry God; they are saints who have sinned, and they rest in the hands of a loving God.

> ALCOHOLICS AND ADDICTS ARE NOT SINNERS IN THE HANDS OF AN ANGRY GOD; THEY ARE SAINTS WHO HAVE SINNED, AND THEY REST IN THE HANDS OF A LOVING GOD.

This is not just a play on words or a minor theological point. And I am not dodging the sin issue. I fully believe that verbalizing a failure identity is counterproductive to what the Holy Spirit wants to affirm. "The Spirit Himself bears witness with our spirit that we are children of God" (Rom. 8:16).

Dear Christian reader, who are you according to the following passages?

> But as many as received Him, to them He gave the right to become *children of God*, even to those who believe in His name (John 1:12, emphasis added).

> To the church of God which is at Corinth, to those who have been sanctified in Christ Jesus, *saints by calling*, with

all who in every place call upon the name of our Lord Jesus Christ, their Lord and ours (1 Cor. 1:2, emphasis added).

For you are all *sons of God* through faith in Christ Jesus. And because you are sons, God has sent forth the Spirit of His Son into our hearts, crying, "Abba! Father!" (Gal. 3:26; 4:6; emphasis added).

You are *a chosen race, a royal priesthood, a holy nation, a people for God's own possession*, that you may proclaim the excellencies of Him who has called you out of darkness into His marvelous light; for you once were not a people, but now you are the people of God; you had not received mercy, but now you have received mercy (1 Pet. 2:9-10, emphasis added).

See how great a love the Father has bestowed upon us, that we should be called *children of God*; and such we are. For this reason the world does not know us, because it did not know Him. Beloved, now we are children of God, and it has not appeared as yet what we shall be. We know that, when He appears, we shall be like Him, because we shall see Him just as He is. And everyone who has this hope fixed on Him purifies himself, just as He is pure (1 John 3:1-3, emphasis added).

First John 3:1-3 reveals a critical reason why knowing our true identity in Christ is so important. People cannot consistently behave in a way that is inconsistent with what they believe about themselves. When people consider themselves losers or alcoholics, their belief can eventually become a self-fulfilling prophecy.

It is not what we do that determines who we are; it is who we are and what we believe about ourselves that determine what we do. In our culture we have a tendency to get our individual identities from the things we do. This is particularly true of men, but it applies to women as well. We are carpenters, truck drivers, teachers, lawyers and engineers. But what happens if we lose our jobs? Do we lose our identities? We tend to apply the same logic to sin. If we sin, we must be sinners. If we burp, are we burpers? If we sneeze, are we sneezers? According to the Bible, we are saints who burp, sneeze and choose to sin. If we are sinners, how would we ever hope to do anything other than commit acts of sin?

We don't call someone Cancer because they have cancer or Chicken Pox when they have chicken pox. Sick people do not stand up in a cancer ward and say, "Hi, I'm Fred, and I am cancerous." A cancer patient could appropriately say, "Hi, I'm Fred, and I have cancer." Fred has a problem, but he is not *the problem*.

Christians have problems, but we are not the problem. If we were, there would be no way to resolve it. We would have to get rid of the Christian in order to get rid of the problem.

Christians can create problems for themselves by living in denial or by not assuming proper responsibility for living a righteous life. A Christian struggling with alcoholism should say, "Hi, I'm Fred, a child of God. Right now I am struggling with sin, and I know that I can resolve this issue and live freely in Christ, because I am 'Dead to sin, but alive to God in Christ Jesus' [Rom. 6:11]."

Why do Christians identify Christians who are struggling with an addiction by the addiction? Have we simply borrowed this practice from the secular world? Unbelievers cannot say they are children of God, because they are not. But I don't think they should identify themselves by their addiction either. They would be better off if they would say something like "Hi, I'm Fred, and I have a major problem with alcohol."

WORKING THE 12-STEP PROGRAM

The 12-step program in which people all over the world put their hopes was originally a Christian program that clearly identified the higher power as the God of the Bible. Participants found their freedom in Christ through genuine repentance and faith in God. Because the program was so effective, other religious groups and those who did not put their faith in God wanted to use it. They thought it was the program itself that set people free. It wasn't. It was God, not some unknown higher power. The non-Christian world adopted the program and secularized it. As a result, many people have been helped to live more responsible lives, and some have been able to achieve sobriety by sheer willpower and with the help of a supportive group. But they haven't become alive and free in Christ.

Many recovery ministers have tried to reclaim the 12 steps as the primary means for recovery. They have identified the higher power as Christ and added Scriptures to each step, but in many cases they are still working the program. I appreciate their efforts, and I don't want to be critical of my brothers and sisters in Christ, but I have some major concerns with their approach.

An Incomplete Message

One of my major concerns is the incomplete message of the program. I don't believe the 12 steps are wrong if each step is understood from a Christian perspective, but as I have already noted, I don't agree with the public pronouncement of a failure identity.

Knowing our identity and position in Christ is critical for overcoming addictive behaviors, and that is glaringly missing in the program. The program has a step to ask for forgiveness, which is important, but it does not have a step to forgive others, which is critical if we want to find our freedom in Christ. Most responsible Christians can easily correct this area of concern.

However, there is another serious oversight that, because of the absence of people's biblical understanding, is not as easy to correct: the spiritual battle that they're in.

A Need for Biblical Understanding

Another concern is the program orientation itself. Christian counseling or recovery in Christ is not a technique that we learn or a program that we follow. Christian counseling is an encounter with God. He is the wonderful counselor, and the only One who can set the captive free and bind up the brokenhearted (see Isa. 9:6; 61:1). He alone grants repentance that leads to the knowledge of the truth, which sets people free (see 2 Tim. 2:24-26).

> TRUTH AS REPRESENTED IN THE PERSON OF CHRIST—NOT PROGRAMS, STRATEGIES OR HUMAN EFFORT—SETS PEOPLE FREE.

Truth as represented in the person of Christ—not programs, strategies or human effort—sets people free. Jesus is the only way, the only truth and the only means by which we can have spiritual life and be set free from the bondage of sin (see John 14:6). Along the same line of reasoning, discipleship is not just following a curriculum or program. Discipleship is the process of building the life of Christ into one another based on the Word of God, which is enabled by His presence. Accepting these distinctions leads to a different orientation in the Christian care of those who are suffering and living in bondage.[1]

To illustrate this point, consider John 15:8: "By this is My Father glorified, that you bear much fruit, and so prove to be My disciples." Without knowing the context, we could easily conclude that we have to bear fruit. Actually we don't; we have to abide in Christ. If we abide in Christ, we will bear fruit. Bearing fruit is the evidence that we are abiding in Christ. Too often we attempt to bear fruit without abiding in Christ. This happens when we work the program. A program does not bear fruit. It cannot set captives free or bind up the brokenhearted.

I am not suggesting that we eliminate all Christian programs and strategies; rather, I am pointing out that even with the best of intentions, programs that don't accommodate the presence of Christ will not be fruitful. When Christ is present, almost any program or strategy will work. But a well-thought-out program or strategy in which Christ is present will bear more fruit than a poorly thought out one.

EMBRACING THE GOOD NEWS

The truth is, Christ is in us, and the realization of this truth is liberating. To his delight, the famous missionary Hudson Taylor discovered this and wrote about it.

> I felt the ingratitude, the danger, the sin of not living nearer to God. I prayed, agonized, fasted, strove, made resolutions, read the Word more diligently, sought more time for meditation—but without avail. Every day, almost every hour, the consciousness of sin oppressed me.
>
> I knew that if only I could abide in Christ all would be well, but I could not.... Each day brought its register of sin and failure, of lack of power. To will was indeed present within me, but how to perform I found not.... Then came the question, is there no rescue? ... I hated

myself, my sin, yet gained no strength against it. . . .

All the time I felt assured that there was in Christ all I needed, but the practical question was—how to get it out. . . . I strove for faith, but it would not come. . . . I prayed for faith, but it came not. What was I to do?

When my agony of soul was at its height, a sentence in a letter . . . was used to remove the scales from my eyes, and the Spirit of God revealed to me the truth of our oneness with Jesus as I had never known it before. "But how to get faith strengthened? Not by striving after faith, but by resting on the faithful One."

As I read, I saw it all! "If we believe not, He abideth faithful." I looked to Jesus and saw . . . that He had said, "I will never leave thee." I thought, "I have striven in vain to rest in Him. I'll strive no more."

I am no better than before. In a sense I do not wish to be. But I am dead, buried with Christ—aye, and risen too! And now Christ lives in me. . . . Do not let us consider Him as far off, when God has made us one with Him, members of His body. Nor should we look upon this experience, these truths, as for a few. They are the birthright of every child of God . . . the only power for deliverance from sin or for true service.[2]

GOING DEEPER

1. Have you committed your life to Christ? If not, what keeps you from making a full commitment to Him?
2. What does Christ's resurrection mean to you as a believer?
3. How will knowing your identity and position in Christ enable you to get out of bondage to sin?
4. What is the difference between a recovery program and an encounter with Christ?

Notes

1. For a more complete discussion of our identity in Christ, read Neil Anderson and Dave Park, *Overcoming Negative Self-Image* (Ventura, CA: Regal Books, 2003). To understand how to include Christ in the counseling process, read Neil Anderson, *Discipleship Counseling* (Ventura, CA: Regal Books, 2003).

2. Hudson Taylor, quoted in Dr. and Mrs. Howard Taylor, *Hudson Taylor's Spiritual Secret* (Chicago, IL: Moody Press, 1990), pp. 158-164.

VICTORY OVER SIN

It is the magician's bargain: give up our souls, get power in return.
But once our souls, that is, our selves, have been given up, the power thus
conferred will not belong to us. We shall in fact be the slaves and
puppets of that to which we have given our souls.

C. S. LEWIS

The same power that brought Christ back from the dead is operative within
those who are Christ's. The resurrection is an ongoing thing.

LEON MORRIS

Several years ago a professor at a secular university invited me to
speak on the subject of Christian morality in the context of marriage and family. The class I addressed was predominantly made
up of young women. There, however, was one male student who

purposely pulled his chair into a corner to protest my presence. He sat and read a newspaper; occasionally he interrupted my speech with a vulgar noise.

A young woman in the class asked me what Christians thought about masturbation. Before I could answer, the young man in the corner piped up: "Well, I masturbate every day!"

"Congratulations," I said. "Can you stop?"

I didn't hear from him again until the end of the class, after everybody else had left. As he walked by me on his way to the door, he said, "Why would I want to stop?"

"That's not what I asked you," I said. "I asked if you could stop. What you think is freedom, really isn't freedom at all—it's just sexual bondage."

MAKING CHOICES

Some people define freedom as the right to do their own thing, to exercise their choices, to be free moral agents. No rules! No regulations! No restrictions! "I can do whatever I want to do," say the libertarians, defending the right to make their own choices. "If I want to have a drink, I'm going to have a drink." They don't seem to have a clue as to how deep their bondage is to sin. Freedom does not lie only in the exercise of choice; it is also always related to the consequences of that choice.

I suppose I am "free" to tell a lie, but wouldn't I be in bondage to that choice? I would have to remember to whom I told the lie and what I told them. I suppose I am "free" to rob a bank, but wouldn't I be in bondage to that act the rest of my life? I would always be looking over my shoulder, wondering if I would be caught. We can choose to drink shots all night, sleep with a prostitute or inject heroin into our body, but we would have to live with the consequences of each choice. The free sex promoted in the '60s led to rampant sexual bondage in the decades that have followed. That is not freedom; that is license—which only leads to bondage. Whether or not we have the right to drink, take drugs or fornicate is not the ultimate issue. The real issue is whether we can stop the behavior.

Anybody who acts as his or her own god is in bondage to the flesh. As a result of the Fall, we were sold into the slave market of sin. Jesus purchased us from the kingdom of darkness and saved us from ourselves.

> Or do you not know that your body is a temple of the Holy Spirit who is in you, whom you have from God, and that you are not your own? For you have been bought with a price: therefore glorify God in your body (1 Cor. 6:19-20).

We are no longer slaves to sin. We are bond servants of the Lord Jesus Christ. Only when we realize this truth and embrace it are

> WE ARE NO LONGER SLAVES TO SIN. WE ARE BOND SERVANTS OF THE LORD JESUS CHRIST.

we able to make the kinds of choices that allow us to live in the freedom that Christ purchased for us at the cross.

EMBRACING FREEDOM IN CHRIST

Freedom is the most practical benefit of being a child of God. Being a servant of sin is bondage. Being a bond servant of Christ means being free in three ways.

Free from the Law

First, we are free from the Law. Galatians 5:1 reads, "It was for freedom that Christ set us free; therefore . . . do not be subject again to a yoke of slavery." Legalists who are driven by the law will feel cursed and condemned all their lives, but those who live by the Spirit have life and liberty: "Now the Lord is the Spirit; and where the Spirit of the Lord is, there is liberty" (2 Cor. 3:17).

Free from the Past

Second, we are free from our past. Writing to the Galatians, Paul put it best:

> Because you are sons, God sent the Spirit of his Son into our hearts, the Spirit who calls out, "Abba, Father." So you are no longer a slave, but a son; and since you are a son, God has made you also an heir. Formerly, when you did not know God, you were slaves to those who by nature are not gods (4:6-8, *NIV*).

As children of God, we are no longer products of what we did yesterday, 10 years ago or at any time in the past; we are primarily products of the work of Christ on the cross. We have a new heritage in our Lord. We are no longer slaves to sin; we are free. Here is an analogy that illustrates my point:

> Slavery in the United States was abolished by the 13th amendment on December 18, 1865. How many slaves were there on December 19? In reality, none, but many still lived like slaves. Many did because they never learned the truth, and others knew and even believed that they were free but chose to live as they had been taught.
>
> Several plantation owners were devastated by this proclamation of emancipation. "We're ruined! Slavery

has been abolished. We've lost the battle to keep our slaves." But their chief spokesman slyly responded, "Not necessarily; as long as these people think they're still slaves, the proclamation of emancipation will have no practical effect. We don't have a legal right over them anymore, but many of them don't know it. Keep your slaves from learning the truth, and your control over them will not even be challenged."

"But what if the news spreads?"

"Don't panic. We have another barrel in our gun. We may not be able to keep them from hearing the news, but we can still keep them from understanding it. They don't call me the father of lies for nothing. We still have the potential to deceive the whole world. Just tell them that they misunderstood the 13th amendment. Tell them that they are going to be free, not that they are free already. The truth they heard is just positional truth, not actual truth. Someday they may receive the benefits, but not now."

"But they'll expect me to say that. They won't believe me."

"Then pick out a few persuasive ones who are convinced that they're still slaves and let them do the talking for you. Remember, most of these free people were born as slaves and have lived like slaves. All we have to do is to deceive them so that they still think like slaves. As long as they continue to do what slaves do, it will not be hard to convince them that they must still be slaves. They will maintain their slave identity because of the things they do. The moment they try to profess that they are no longer slaves, just whisper in their ear, 'How can you even think you are no longer a slave when you are still doing things that slaves do?' After all, we have the capacity to accuse the brethren day and night."

Years later, many had still not heard the wonderful news that they had been freed, so naturally they continued to live the way they had always lived. Some had heard the good news, but they evaluated it by what they were presently doing and feeling. They reasoned, *I'm still living in bondage, doing the same things I have always done. My experience tells me that I must not be free. I'm feeling the same way I was before the proclamation, so it must not be true. After all, your feelings always tell the truth.* So they continued to live according to how they felt, not wanting to be hypocrites!

One former slave heard the good news and received it with great joy. He checked out the validity of the proclamation and found out that the highest of all authorities had originated the decree. Not only that, but it personally cost the authority a tremendous price, which He willingly paid, so that he could be free. His life was transformed. He correctly reasoned that it would be hypocritical to believe his feelings and not believe the truth. Determined to live by what he knew to be true, his experiences began to change rather dramatically. He realized that his old master had no authority over him and did not need to be obeyed. He gladly served the One who set him free.[1]

Free from Sin

Third, we are "freed from sin" (Rom. 6:7).

One of my students once inquired, "Are you telling me that I don't have to sin?"

"Where did you get the idea that you have to sin?" I asked.

In his Gospel, John wrote, "My dear children, I write this to you so that you will not sin. But if anybody does sin, we have one who speaks to the Father in our defense—Jesus Christ, the Righteous One" (1 John 2:1, *NIV*). Obviously, maturity factors into our ability to stand against sin, but what an incredible sense of defeat we would have if we believed that we had to sin, while at the same time God commands us to be holy (see 1 Pet. 1:15-16).

Those who are living in bondage are caught in a web of faulty thinking: *God, You made me this way and now You condemn me for it! The Christian life is impossible!* When those people fail, they proclaim, "I'm only human!"

People who struggle with chemical and sexual addictions lead this parade of despair. They entertain thoughts such as, *I'm different from others. Christianity works for others but it doesn't work for me. Maybe I'm not a Christian. God doesn't love me. How could He? I'm such a failure. I'm just a miserable sinner with no hope of ever breaking the chains of alcoholism.* What a pack of lies! People who think like this are still living like slaves because they are still thinking like slaves.

Examining the Truth

To live free in Christ, we must know the Christian emancipation proclamation found in Romans 6:1-11. Before we look at this liberating text, which explains our position in Christ, let me clarify some simple principles of biblical interpretation. When we come to a commandment in the Bible, the only proper response is to obey it. If Scripture is trying to declare something that is true, our only proper response is to believe it. If we read a promise in the Word of God, we should claim it. It is a simple concept, but it is critical to understand if we are going to move deeper into Romans 6:1-11. Our tendency is to read this passage and ask, *How do I do that?* Paul's explanation of our relationship to sin is not something we do; it is something we believe—and believing this truth will set us free.

The Greek language used in the original New Testament texts is very precise when it comes to verbs. We can know when a verb is past, present or future tense, and whether a verb is describing continuous action or a point in time. However, we don't need to know Greek to appreciate what the Word of God declares, because English translations closely match the meaning in Greek. But I'm going to try to make the truth of this text even clearer. As we examine the truth in Romans 6:1-11, I encourage you to pray: Ask the Holy Spirit, who is the Spirit of truth, to protect your mind and enable you to understand the full meaning of this passage.

Dead to Sin

> What shall we say, then? Shall we go on sinning so that grace may increase? By no means! We died to sin; how can we live in it any longer? (Rom. 6:1-2, *NIV*).

You may be tempted to ask, *How do I do that? How do I die to sin?* We can't, because we have already died to sin. The verb is past tense. We cannot do what has already been done for us by Christ. *But I don't feel dead to sin, and frankly I am still sinning.* Remember, it is not what we do that determines who we are. Just

> IT'S WHAT WE BELIEVE THAT'S GOING TO SET US FREE, NOT WHAT WE FEEL.

set your feelings aside for a few verses. It's what we believe that's going to set us free, not what we feel. God's Word is true whether we choose to believe it or not. Believing the Word of God doesn't make it true. His Word is true; therefore, we believe it.

A pastor shared with me that for 22 years in his Christian experience he had struggled with sin. "It's been one trial after another, and I think I've finally found the answer," he said. "I was reading Colossians 3:3 [NIV], 'For you died, and your life is now hidden with Christ in God.' That's the key isn't it?"

I assured him that I thought it was the key. Then he asked how he could, according to Colossians 3:3, die and have his life hidden in Christ. I was surprised by his question. For 22 years this dear man had been desperately trying to become somebody he already is. Many Christians, especially those mired in bondage, have lived the same way.

Identified with Christ

Paul's argument in Romans 6:1-11 is twofold. First, if we identify with the death and burial of Christ, we also identify with His resurrection and ascension. We will live in defeat if we believe only half of the gospel message. Not only are we free from bondage, but we are also seated with Christ in the heavenlies (see Eph. 2:6). From this position we have the authority and power to live the Christian life. Jesus didn't simply come to Earth to die for our sins; He came to give us life—therefore, every child of God is spiritually alive in Christ. Paul clearly identified every believer with Christ:

Eternal life.

In His death	see Romans 6:3,6; Galatians 2:20; Colossians 3:1-3
In His burial	see Romans 6:4
In His resurrection	see Romans 6:5,8,11
In His ascension	see Ephesians 2:6
In His life	see Romans 5:10-11
In His power	see Ephesians 1:19-20
In His inheritance	see Romans 8:16-17; Ephesians 1:11-12

United with Christ

The second part of Paul's argument is that death no longer has any power over us; therefore, neither does sin. We will see how and why that is true when we get to those verses. Returning to his first argument, let's continue in Romans 6:

> Or don't you know that all of us who were baptized into Christ Jesus were baptized into his death? (v. 3, *NIV*).

Are you still wondering, *How do I do that?* The answer is the same: We can't, because we already have been baptized into Christ Jesus.[2] It is futile to seek something that the Bible affirms we already have. "For we were all baptized by one Spirit into one body" (1 Cor. 12:13, *NIV*). The phrase "we were" is past tense. It has already happened for the believer.

Let's continue with verses 4 and 5 (*NIV*):

> In order that, just as Christ was raised from the dead through the glory of the Father, we too may live a new life. If we have been united with him like this in his death, we will certainly also be united with him in his resurrection.

Have we been united with Him? Absolutely! Those who study the original language say the syntax and verb form create a first-class conditional clause. This means that this passage can literally be read: For if we have become united with Him in the likeness of His death *and we have*, we shall also be in the likeness of His resurrection.

We celebrate Christ's resurrection on Easter, not just His death on Good Friday. We receive the resurrected life of Christ within us the moment we are born again. Notice how Paul developed the whole gospel:

But God demonstrates his own love for us in this: While we were still sinners, Christ died for us (Rom. 5:8, *NIV*).

This is great! God loves us. But is that all there is to the gospel? No! Read on:

Since we have now been justified by his blood, how *much more* shall we be saved from God's wrath through him! (5:9, *NIV*, emphasis added).

This is terrific! We are not going to hell. But is that the entire truth of the gospel? No! Read on:

For if, when we were God's enemies, we were reconciled to him through the death of his Son, how *much more,* having been reconciled, shall we be saved through his life! (5:10, *NIV*, emphasis added).

This is incredible! We have been saved by His life, and eternal life is not merely something we get when we die—we are alive in Christ right now. But is that the complete gospel message? No! Read on:

Not only is this so, but we also rejoice in God through our Lord Jesus Christ, through whom we have now received reconciliation (5:11, *NIV*, emphasis added).

This reconciliation assures us that our soul is in union with God, and that is what it means to be spiritually alive. Paul told us there is even more:

For if by the transgression of the one, death reigned through the one, much more those who receive the abundance of grace and of the gift of righteousness will reign in life through the One, Jesus Christ (5:17).

CHOOSING TO BELIEVE THE TRUTH

Now return to Romans 6:6 (*NIV*): "For we know that our old self was crucified with him." Are you still asking yourself, *How do I do that*? This is not something we can do. This is something we can only know and believe. This is a question of knowledge, not experience. The text does not declare: "For we must do." It is clear: "For we know." Many people try desperately to put the old self (old man) to death, yet they fail. Why? Because the old self is already dead! We cannot do for ourselves what God has already done for us.

So many people who fail in their Christian experience begin to reason, *What experience must I have in order for this to be true?* With this thinking, we will never see victory! The only experience that had to happen in order for this verse to be true

> WE CAN'T SAVE OURSELVES, AND WE CAN'T USE HUMAN EFFORT TO OVERCOME THE PENALTY OF DEATH AND THE POWER OF SIN. ONLY GOD CAN DO THAT FOR US—AND HE DID.

occurred nearly 2,000 years ago on the Cross, and the only way we can enter into that experience today is by faith. We can't save ourselves, and we can't use human effort to overcome the penalty of death and the power of sin. Only God can do that for us—and He did.

Some people have asserted that this teaching is just positional truth, implying that there is little or no present-day benefit for being alive in Christ. What a tragic conclusion that is. In our industrialized, how-to Western world we often try to do for ourselves what only Christ can do and which He has already done for us. That will never work. No matter how we feel or how seriously we are failing in our Christian experience, we must choose to believe the truth and then walk accordingly by faith. When we do, the truth of this passage becomes evident in our experience. Trying to make it true by our experience will only lead to defeat. We are saved and sanctified by faith, not by works.

I don't do the things I do with the hope that God may someday accept me. I'm accepted in the beloved; that is why I do the things that I do. I don't labor in the vineyard with the hope that God may someday love me; God loves me and, therefore, I labor in the vineyard. Remember, it is not what we do that determines who we are; it is who we are and what we believe that determine what we do. Beloved, you are a child of God (see 1 John 3:2).

Let's look again at Romans 6:6 (*NIV*):

> For we know that our old self was crucified with him so that the body of sin might be done away with, that we should no longer be slaves to sin.

The latter part of this verse refers to our physical body, which I discuss in the following chapter. But there is something else that is important here: We are saved and sanctified by faith. To believe otherwise is foolish and a deceptive trick of the devil, according to Paul:

You foolish Galatians! Who has bewitched you? . . . Did you receive the Spirit by observing the law, or by believing what you heard? Are you so foolish? After beginning with the Spirit, are you now trying to attain your goal by human effort? (Gal. 3:1-3, *NIV*).

Christians living in bondage to sin are believing the Galatian heresy.

Paul continued in Romans 6:7 (*NIV*): "Anyone who has died has been freed from sin." Have you died with Christ? Then you are freed from sin. You are probably thinking, *I don't feel free from sin*. If we only believe what we feel, we will never live victorious lives.

Most of us wake up some mornings and feel alive to sin and dead to Christ. But that's just the way we feel. If we believed what we felt and lived that way the rest of the day, what kind of a day would we have? It would be a bad day! I have learned to get up in the morning and say, "Thank You, Lord, for another day. I deserved eternal damnation, but You gave me eternal life. I now ask You to fill me with Your Holy Spirit, and I choose to walk by faith today regardless of how I feel. I realize that I will face many temptations, but I choose to take every thought captive to the obedience of Christ and to think upon that which is true and right."

More than once, the Lord replied to me, "Be it done to you according to how you believe."

Having the right faith foundation is vital. The alternative can be fatal. There is no greater sin than the sin of unbelief. "Everything that does not come from faith is sin" (Rom. 14:23, *NIV*). If we choose to believe a lie, we will live a lie; but if we choose to believe the truth, we will live fruitful lives by faith in the power of the Holy Spirit.

COUNTING OURSELVES DEAD TO SIN AND ALIVE TO GOD

Paul continued in Romans 6:8-9 (*NIV*):

> Now if we died with Christ, we believe that we will also live with him. For we know that since Christ was raised from the dead, he cannot die again; death no longer has mastery over him.

Does death have mastery over you? Absolutely not!

> "Death has been swallowed up in victory." "Where, O death, is your victory? Where, O death, is your sting?" The sting of death is sin, and the power of sin is the law. But thanks be to God! He gives us the victory through our Lord Jesus Christ (1 Cor. 15:54-57, *NIV*).

Paul argued that if death has no mastery over us, then neither does sin. "The death he died, he died to sin once for all; but the life he lives, he lives to God" (Rom. 6:10, *NIV*). This was accomplished when "God made him who had no sin to be sin for us, so that *in him* we might become the righteousness of God" (2 Cor. 5:21, *NIV*, emphasis added). When Jesus went to the cross, all the sins of the world were on Him. When the spikes were nailed into His hands and feet, He carried the weight of all of our sins. But when He was resurrected, there was not a single sin on Him. As He sits at the right hand of the Father, there are not any sins on Him. He has triumphed over sin and death. He died to sin once for all. Many accept the truth that Christ died for the sins we have already committed, but what if we sin again in the future? At the moment Christ died for all of our sins, how many of our sins were at that moment future sins? *They all were.*

Knowing that our past, present and future sins have already been forgiven, or atoned for, is not a license to sin; rather, it is a gracious means not to sin.

KNOWING THAT OUR PAST, PRESENT AND FUTURE SINS HAVE ALREADY BEEN FORGIVEN, OR ATONED FOR, IS NOT A LICENSE TO SIN; RATHER, IT IS A GRACIOUS MEANS NOT TO SIN.

How should we respond to this truth? Paul continued in Romans 6:11 (*NIV*):

> In the same way, count yourselves dead to sin but alive to God *in Christ Jesus* (emphasis added).

We do not make ourselves dead to sin by considering ourselves so. We consider ourselves dead to sin because God says it is already true. I remember ministering to a number of people who were struggling with this passage. The *New King James Version* reads, "Reckon yourselves to be dead indeed to sin." I told the people who were struggling that if they thought it was the reckoning that made them dead to sin, they would reckon themselves into a wreck. We can't make ourselves dead to sin; only God can do that and He has. Paul was saying that we have to keep on choosing to believe by faith what God says is true, even though all our feelings may be indicating the opposite. The verb "count," or "reckon," is present tense. In other words, we must continuously believe the truth, which is parallel to the idea of abiding in Christ (see John 15:1-8), which is basically the same as walking by the Spirit (see Gal. 5:16). When we walk by the Spirit, we will not carry out the desires of the flesh.

Death is the ending of a relationship, not of existence itself. Throughout the Bible, the word "life" means "to be in union with," and the word "death" means "separation from." As we have already noted, when Adam sinned, he died spiritually. He didn't pass out of existence. In fact, he remained physically alive for more than 900 years. His soul, however, was separated from God. When we are born again, we become spiritually alive. Our soul is in union with God. We are alive in Christ. The phrase "in Christ," or "in Him," is one of the most frequently used prepositional phrases in the New Testament.

FINDING VICTORY OVER TEMPTATION

When we die to sin, does sin itself pass out of existence? No! Has the power of sin died? No! It is still strong and still appealing. However, when sin makes its appeal, we have the power to say no to it because our relationship with sin ended when the Lord "rescued us from the dominion of darkness and brought us into the kingdom of the Son he loves" (Col. 1:13, *NIV*). In Romans 8:1-2 (*NIV*), Paul explained how this is possible:

> Therefore, there is now no condemnation for those who are in Christ Jesus, because through Christ Jesus the law of the Spirit of life set me free from the law of sin and death.

Is the law of sin and death still operative? Yes, because it is a law. We cannot do away with a law, but we can overcome an existing law with a law greater than it, namely, the law of the Spirit of life. For instance, can we as mere mortals fly by our own power? No, because the law of gravity will keep us bound to Earth. But we can fly if we unite ourselves with a power greater than gravity. As long as we remain *in* the airplane and operate according to that power, we can fly. On the other hand, if we step out of that airplane, we will quickly find that the law of gravity is still in effect. Down we go!

The law of sin and death is still alive, still operative, still powerful and still making its appeal. But we don't have to submit to it. As long as we walk (live) by the Spirit, we will not carry out the desires of the flesh (see Gal. 5:16). We must "be strong in the Lord and in his mighty power" (Eph. 6:10, *NIV*). The moment we stop being dependent on the Lord and choose to walk by the flesh, we will crash and burn. The moment we think we can stand on our own, we are setting ourselves up for a fall. "Pride goes before destruction, a haughty spirit before a fall" (Prov. 16:18, *NIV*).

The devil attempts to get us to live our lives independently of God.

> So, if you think you are standing firm, be careful that you don't fall! No temptation has seized you except what is common to man. And God is faithful; he will not let you be tempted beyond what you can bear. But when you are tempted, he will also provide a way out so that you can stand up under it (1 Cor. 10:12-13, *NIV*).

Should we succumb to the devil's temptation or be deceived by him? Should we believe his lies? No! Instead, we should repent for our ways, renounce the lies and return to our loving Father who has forgiven us of our sins and who will cleanse us.

If you are mired in addiction to alcohol, sex or drugs, you are probably thinking, *This all sounds good and I want to believe it, but I am still struggling*. You're probably thinking this because of the other truths that need to be understood: The pleasures of sin "wage war in your members" (Jas. 4:1), and there is a battle going on for your mind. How to understand and win those battles is the subject of the subsequent chapters.

Watchman Nee came to realize the truth presented by Paul in Romans 6:1-11, and it literally set him free. I close this chapter with his testimony:

> For years after my conversion, I had been taught to reckon. . . . The more I reckoned that I was dead to sin, the more alive I clearly was. I simply could not believe myself dead, and I could not produce the death. Whenever I sought help from others, I was told to read Romans 6:1-11, and the more I read Romans 6:1-11, and tried to reckon, the further away death was: I could not get at it. I fully appreciated the teaching that I must reckon, but I could not make out why nothing resulted from it. I have to confess that for months I was troubled. I said to the Lord, "If this is not clear, if I cannot be brought to see this which is so fundamental, I will cease to do anything. I will not preach anymore; I will not go out to serve Thee any more; I want first of all to get thoroughly clear here." For months I was seeking, and at times I fasted, but nothing came through.
>
> I remember one morning . . . I said, "Lord, open my eyes!" And then in a flash I saw it. I saw my oneness with Christ. I saw that I was *in Him*, and that when He died, I died. I saw that the question of my death was a matter of the past and not of the future, and that I was just as truly dead as He was because I was *in Him* when He died. The whole thing had dawned upon me. I was carried away with such joy at this great discovery that I jumped from

my chair and cried, "Praise the Lord, I am dead!" I ran downstairs and met one of the brothers helping in the kitchen and laid hold of him. "Brother," I said, "do you know that I have died?" I must admit he looked puzzled. "What do you mean?" he said, so I went on: "Do you not know that Christ has died? Do you not know that I died with Him? Do you not know that my death is no less truly a fact than His?"[3]

GOING DEEPER

1. How does the natural person define freedom? How does that differ from the freedom we can enjoy in Christ?
2. Identify some of the faulty thinking of people who live in bondage. Why is their reasoning flawed? What would be the proper thinking in light of what Christ has done for us?
3. What is eternal life? When do you receive it (as a Christian)?
4. What is death? Why is it important to understand this as a believer?

Notes

1. This illustration was adapted from Jamie Lash's article "Enslaved to My Self-Image," which was originally published by Victory Seminar Ministries, Dallas, Texas. Used by permission.

2. The ordinance of water baptism is typically understood to be the symbolic representation of what has already been accomplished by Christ. Saint Augustine called it a visible form of an invisible grace. It is a public identification with the death, burial and resurrection of the Lord Jesus Christ. Those who practice infant baptism, however, understand the ordinance to be symbolic of the Holy Spirit's coming upon Christ. They would, then, sprinkle water on the head as opposed to immersing the body. Both look to Scripture for the basis of their practice, and both see it as an identification with Christ. The passage we are examining, however, deals with our spiritual baptism into Christ, of which the external ordinance practiced by your church and mine is a symbol.

3. Watchman Nee, *The Normal Christian Life* (Wheaton, IL: Tyndale House Publishers, 1977), pp. 64-65.

THE WAR IN OUR MEMBERS

The strength for our conquering and victory is drawn continually from Christ.
The Bible does not teach that sin is completely eradicated from the Christian in
this life, but it does teach that sin shall no longer reign over you. The strength and
power of sin have been broken. The Christian now has the resources available to
live above and beyond this world. It is like the little girl who said that when the
devil came knocking with a temptation, she just sent Jesus to the door.

BILLY GRAHAM

There once was a mule that was walking in the wrong direction.
As he strolled along, he had more and more problems. He was a
stubborn mule; so despite the difficulty, he wouldn't admit he
was headed in the wrong direction—instead he walked faster. He

also wasn't taking the time to eat a balanced meal of oats and hay. To make matters worse, the mule started drinking contaminated water that temporarily solved one problem—his thirst. Then he started running with some bad mules that introduced him to some other kinds of contaminated water. Finally, the stubborn mule fell over in utter defeat and exhaustion.

It wasn't long before some well-meaning mules came along. One of the helpful mules concluded that contaminated water had contributed to the stubborn mule's downfall, so he cut off the supply. But the stubborn mule still lay there. Another well-meaning mule correctly perceived that the sick mule had been going in the wrong direction, so he grabbed that old mule by the tail and turned him around; but the stubborn mule still lay there. Another in the well-meaning group was concerned about the stubborn mule's reputation and appearance, so he hosed off the defeated mule and cleaned him up on the outside. But the stubborn mule still lay there. All those well-intentioned efforts were commendable, but that old mule was still the same stubborn mule he had always been. He needed a new life that would transform him and give him the power to get up and walk in the right direction.

GLORIFYING GOD IN OUR BODY

If we are ever to tap into the treasure trove of God's plan for our lives, we must understand some basic principles. God created us to glorify Him in our body (see 1 Cor. 6:20). The glory of God is a manifestation of His presence. Essentially, Christians are called to manifest the presence of God in this world. Jesus said, "By this is My Father glorified, that you bear much fruit, and so prove to be My disciples" (John 15:8). The only way that we can do this is by abiding in Christ. We cannot do for ourselves what Christ has already done for us, but we can choose to repent of our old self-centered ways, choose the right way and start living by faith according to what God says is true. We can do all of this if we are enabled by the life of Christ within us.

In the last chapter we looked at what God has done for us and how we must accept that as truth and live accordingly by faith. In this chapter, let's focus on what our responsibility is. Before we do, let me clarify that what follows in this chapter will not be effective in your life if you do not first believe what Paul taught in Romans 6:1-11. Truth sets us free, and believing the truth is what determines responsible behavior.

Now let's continue with Romans 6:12 (*NIV*): "Therefore do not let sin reign in your mortal body so that you obey its evil desires." It is our responsibility not to allow sin to reign in our mortal body. I have never believed, nor taught, that we can excuse ourselves with a devil-made-me-do-it attitude. Nor can we say anybody else made us do it. We are responsible for our own attitudes and actions. What do we have to do or not do to ensure that sin does not reign in our mortal body? Paul answered in verse 13 (*NIV*):

Do not offer the parts of your body to sin, as instruments of wickedness, but rather offer yourselves to God, as those who have been brought from death to life; and offer the parts of your body to him as instruments of righteousness.

There is only one negative action that we must avoid, but two positive actions that we must take. Let's first consider the instruction about the negative action. We are not to use our body in any way that would serve sin. If we do, we will allow sin to reign (rule) in our physical body. James wrote, "What is the source of quarrels and conflicts among you? Is not the source your pleasures that wage war in your members [physical body]?" (Jas. 4:1).

Our Selves and Our Bodies

On the positive side, we are told to consciously offer ("present," *NIV*) *ourselves* to God, because we belong to Him. We are also to offer, or present, *our bodies* to God as instruments of righteousness. Paul separated our selves from our bodies. Why?

Our selves are who we essentially are, that part of us that will be present with the Lord when we are separated from our body. In our culture we have a tendency to derive our identity from the things we do, and we identify one another by our physical bodies. That would be necessary if we were only natural people. As children of God, however, we have a whole new identity: "Therefore from now on we recognize no man according to the flesh" (2 Cor. 5:16). Paul acknowledged that we long "to be clothed with our dwelling from heaven" (2 Cor. 5:2), but as long as we are still in this earthly tent (meaning our physical body), we groan because we do not want to be unclothed. I don't know about your tent, but my tent pegs are coming up, the seams are getting frayed,

> WHEN WE DIE PHYSICALLY, WE WILL JETTISON OUR OLD EARTH SUITS. WE WILL BE ABSENT FROM OUR BODIES AND PRESENT WITH THE LORD.

and the zipper doesn't work very well anymore. The carcass of this old mule isn't in as good of a shape as it was in the days of my youth! My hope, however, isn't in the eternal preservation of my outer man. My hope is in the facts that I'm being renewed in the inner man day by day, even though the "outer man is decaying"

(2 Cor. 4:16), and that someday I will receive a resurrected body.

When we die physically, we will jettison our old Earth suits. We will be absent from our bodies and present with the Lord (see 2 Cor. 5:8). As long as we serve the Lord on planet Earth, however, we need our physical body. Paul wrote, "The body that is sown is perishable, it is raised imperishable; it is sown in dishonor, it is raised in glory; it is sown in weakness, it is raised in power; it is sown a natural body, it is raised a spiritual body" (1 Cor. 15:42-44, *NIV*). Our inner man will live forever with our heavenly Father, but our body will return to dust, because "flesh and blood cannot inherit the kingdom of God" (1 Cor. 15:50).

All that is mortal is also corruptible. Our physical body is not by nature evil, but it is amoral, or neutral. So what are we to do about the neutral disposition of our body? We are told to present it as an instrument of righteousness. "Present" means "to put at the disposal of." An instrument can be anything that the Lord has entrusted to us. The Lord commands us to be good stewards of our body and to use it only as an instrument of righteousness.

Members of Christ Himself

Let's apply this line of thinking and what Paul wrote in 1 Corinthians 6:13-20 (*NIV*) to the problem of sexual bondage:

> The body is not meant for sexual immorality, but for the Lord, and the Lord for the body. By His power God raised the Lord from the dead, and he will raise us also. Do you not know that your bodies are members of Christ himself? Shall I then take the members of Christ and unite them with a prostitute? Never! Do you not know that he who unites himself with a prostitute is one with her in body? For it is said, "The two will become one flesh." But he who unites himself with the Lord is

one with him in spirit. Flee from sexual immorality. All other sins a man commits are outside his body, but he who sins sexually sins against his own body. Do you not know that your body is a temple of the Holy Spirit, who is in you, whom you have received from God? You are not your own; you were bought at a price. Therefore honor God with your body.

This passage teaches that we have more than a spiritual union with God. Our body is a member of Christ Himself. Romans 8:11 (*NIV*) declares,

> If the Spirit of him who raised Jesus from the dead is liv-ing in you, he who raised Christ from the dead will also give life to your mortal bodies through his Spirit, who lives in you.

Our body is a temple (dwelling place) of God because His Spirit dwells in us. To use our body for sexual immorality is to defile the temple of God.

It is hard for us to fully appreciate the moral outrage of unit-ing a member of Christ with a prostitute. It would be like Antiochus Epiphanes slaughtering a pig on the altar after declaring Mosaic ceremonies illegal and then erecting a statue of Zeus in the holy place of the Temple. Can you imagine how God's people must have felt when that happened in the second century before Christ? Many were martyred as they attempted to stop Antiochus from defiling the Temple. As Christians, we should be offended when people suggest that Jesus was sexually intimate with Mary Magdalene. We should also be offended when people suggest that Jesus masturbated or was a drunkard.

Jesus was fully God and also fully man. In His humanity, Jesus took on the sexual identity of a man and was tempted in all ways we are tempted—but He never sinned. He never allowed Himself even to entertain thoughts contrary to the will of God. Therefore, sin never had any roots in His soul. His earthly body was not meant for sexual immorality and neither is ours. If our eyes were fully open to the reality of the spiritual world and if we knew what the consequences would be when we sinned against our own bodies, we would flee from all sexual immorality.

There is no way that we can commit a sexual sin and not use our body, including our brain, as an instrument of unrighteousness. When we commit a sexual sin, we allow sin to reign in our mortal body! When this happens, are we still united with the Lord? Yes. We are still joined with Him because He will never leave us nor forsake us. We would not lose our salvation, but the sinful act would certainly have an effect on the degree of freedom that we experience.

> For you were called to freedom, brethren; only do not turn your freedom into an opportunity for the flesh, but through love serve one another (Gal. 5:13).

What happens when a child of God, who is united with the Lord and one in spirit with Him, unites with a prostitute? They become one flesh. Somehow they bond together.

Have you ever heard of a nice Christian girl who has gotten sexually involved with an immoral man and continued in an unhealthy relationship for years? Even her friends try to tell her "He's no good for you." Mom and Dad abhor the idea that he could be a future son-in-law. But the girl won't listen to anyone, so everyone prays that she will someday come to her senses. Even though he treats her badly, she won't leave him. Why not? Because they have bonded. They have become one flesh. Even if she were to leave him, she would not be free of him.

BREAKING SEXUAL (AND OTHER TYPES OF) BONDAGE

At Freedom in Christ Ministries, we have learned over the years that such a strong bond must be broken through complete repentance. In our discipleship counseling, we encourage the counselees to ask the Lord to reveal to their mind every sexual way their body has been used as an instrument of unrighteousness.

When hurting Christians first share their stories, it is common for them to only reveal one or two sexual experiences; but when they sincerely pray in this way, out come all of the other sexual experiences that they had not intended to share. We don't encourage this confession because we want to hear about all their sexual escapades—frankly, we don't want to hear any of them. Rather, we listen for their sakes, because we really want them to experience their freedom in Christ.

As the Lord brings every sexual sin to their mind, we encourage them to renounce those uses of their body with (the person's name) and ask the Lord to break the bond. Then we have them submit their body to God and reserve the sexual use of their body for their spouse only.

In Romans 12:1, Paul urged us to present our body as a living sacrifice "by the mercies of God." Repentance means that we are *turning away from* something that is wrong and *turning to* something that is right. It is not enough for us to acknowledge a lie; we must also choose to believe, accept and follow the truth. To renounce something as wrong is only the first half of repentance. To make it complete, we have to announce what is right. Paul instructed us not to use our body as an instrument of unrighteousness, but he didn't end there. We must also commit our selves and our bodies to God as instruments of righteousness.

After years of helping people find their freedom in Christ, we have observed several patterns in people who have been in sexual bondage. To begin with, promiscuity before marriage seems to lead to a lack of sexual fulfillment after marriage. If the sexual experiences prior to marriage were consensual, the bondage only increased as the people attempted to satisfy their lusts. If the sexual experiences weren't consensual (by that I mean one person went along with it but didn't really want to, or it was rape or incest), women tend to shut down sexually. No matter what the

> PROMISCUITY BEFORE MARRIAGE
> SEEMS TO LEAD TO A LACK
> OF SEXUAL FULFILLMENT
> AFTER MARRIAGE.

cause prior to marriage, once a couple marries, the wife doesn't seem to enjoy sex and the husband doesn't seem to be satisfied with it. I have counseled many wives who can't stand to be touched. They lack the freedom to enter into a loving and mutual expression of love and trust. Some are repulsed by the idea until they break the bondage that comes from having had sex outside of the will of God. They break the bondage by renouncing the previous sexual use of their body, committing themselves and their body to God as a living sacrifice and reserving the sexual use of their body for their spouse only. If they have forgiven from their heart, repentance is complete, and they are free to relate to God and others in a responsible way.

In the cases of rape and incest, others have forcibly caused them to use their body as an instrument of unrighteousness. Tragically, they have become one flesh. I want to scream "Not fair" when sick people defile temples against the will of people who are trying to use their body to glorify God. It's not fair. It's sick, but we live in a sick world. It is no different from Antiochus's defiling the Temple against the will of those who died trying to save it. The good news is that we can be free from such violations. We can renounce those uses of our body, submit to God and resist the devil (see Jas. 4:7). Then we can, and must, forgive those who have abused us, if we want to experience freedom from our past.

Sexual bondage, alcoholism and drug addiction are often intertwined. Rare is the liquor store that doesn't sell pornography. The deep need for acceptance drives many to the counterfeit world of illicit sex, drugs and alcoholism. Alcohol and drugs dull the conscience and impair judgment, which leads to many regrettable sexual escapades. Substance abuse is also a violation of God's temple. Paul's admonition was "Do not get drunk with wine, for that is dissipation, but be filled with the Spirit" (Eph. 5:18). Drunkenness does more than damage the body; it leads to other forms of immorality. "Dissipation" (*asotia*) means "debauchery" or "extreme indulgence in sensuality."[1] It is the wild living of the prodigal son (see Luke 15:13). It is the extravagant squandering of money and the intemperate feeding of physical appetites.

BEING FILLED WITH THE HOLY SPIRIT

Paul's alternative to getting drunk was not abstinence. It is not enough to stop drinking contaminated water. We have to be filled with the Spirit, who will lead us into all truth and will enable us to walk in the right direction. The most inadequate secular treatments for alcohol and drug abuse are those that proudly advertise "No counseling." Such behavioral modification programs will hospitalize addicts for a short period of time and supply them with another drug that causes them to vomit whenever they drink alcohol. Incredible! Nothing is solved. The dissipated mule is still dissipated *and* still facing the wrong direction. The administrators at these centers will say, "At least the mule isn't drinking any more contaminated water." Whoopee!

Let me try to put all of this in context by looking at the bigger picture. In the Old Testament, the sin offering was a blood offering. The blood was drained from the carcass, and the carcass was taken out of the compound and disposed of. Only the blood was sacrificed for the sin offering.

Who is our sin offering? It is the Lord Jesus Christ, of course. "Without shedding of blood there is no forgiveness" (Heb. 9:22). After He shed His blood for us on the cross, His body was taken down and buried. But it didn't stay buried for long, praise the Lord.

Under the Old Testament sacrificial system, a burnt offering was also required. In Hebrew, "burnt" literally means "that which ascends." The burnt offering, unlike the sin offering, was totally consumed on the altar—blood, carcass, everything.

Who is the burnt offering today? We are! Paul wrote, "Therefore, I urge you, brothers, in view of God's mercy, to offer your bodies as living sacrifices, holy and pleasing to God—this is your spiritual act of worship" (Rom. 12:1, *NIV*). It's great that our sins are forgiven—Christ did that for us. But if we want to live victoriously in Christ, then we must present to God our selves and our bodies as instruments of righteousness. To live a liberated life in Christ, we have to be filled with the Holy Spirit.

Under the leadership of Hezekiah, a tremendous revival broke out in the Old Testament (see 2 Chron. 29). First, he cleaned out the Temple and prepared it for worship. What a beautiful picture of repentance! In the New Testament, we are the temple of God. Next, Hezekiah consecrated the priests. Every believer is a priest under the New Covenant. Therefore, consecrating the priests is consistent with Paul's instruction to "present yourselves to God" (Rom. 6:13). Third, Hezekiah ordered the blood offering. Nothing noticeable happened externally, but everyone's sins were forgiven. Finally, "Hezekiah gave the order to sacrifice the burnt offering on the altar. As the offering began, singing to the LORD began also" (2 Chron. 29:27, *NIV*). Under the leadership of King David, 4,000 musicians had been dedicated for offering music in the Tabernacle day and night (see 1 Chron. 16:39-42). Then, under Hezekiah, the music began again.

> AS CHRISTIANS, WE SHOULD HAVE MANY JOYOUS SONGS IN OUR HEARTS; THE MELODIES OF THE LORD SHOULD CONSTANTLY FILL OUR TEMPLES!

Let's read Ephesians 5:18 (*NIV*) again: "Do not get drunk on wine, which leads to debauchery. Instead, be filled with the Spirit." In other words, don't defile the temple of God with wine. That would be debauchery. Instead, we are to let the Spirit of God rule in our hearts and to let the music begin:

> Speak to one another with psalms, hymns and spiritual songs. Sing and make music in your heart to the Lord, always giving thanks to God the Father for everything (Eph. 5:19-20).

Many people sing when they are drunk but not to the glory of God. Some have songs that sound more like funeral dirges.

What's worse is that some Christians don't seem to have any songs in their hearts. I can't imagine this. As Christians, we should have many joyous songs in our hearts; the melodies of the Lord should constantly fill our temples!

GOING DEEPER

1. How can we prevent sin from reigning in our mortal bodies? What is the difference between an act of sin and sin that reigns in our lives?
2. How do we use our bodies as tools for unrighteousness?
3. What is holy sex? How does the unrighteous use of our bodies affect holy sex for men and women? How does the unrighteous use of our bodies affect marriage?
4. What was Paul's alternative to getting drunk? Why is this an important concept in overcoming an addiction?

Note
1. *Merriam-Webster's Collegiate Dictionary*, 10th ed., s.v. "dissipation" and "debauchery."

CHAPTER 7

SEPARATING OURSELVES FROM SIN

We prayed a lot. . . . I'm a free man now. . . . Every once in a while I meet a youngster who knows I used to be a drug addict, as he is now. He asks what he can do to kick the habit. I tell him what I've learned: "Give God's temple, your body, back to Him. The alternative is death."

JOHNNY CASH

What would it be like if we used our body as an instrument of unrighteousness and allowed sin to reign in our mortal body? Paul painted a clear picture in Romans 7:15-25. Let's be a fly on the wall as a pastor dialogues through this passage with someone who is caught in the sin-confess, sin-confess, sin-confess cycle of chemical and sexual addiction.

> *Randy:* I can't keep living like this. I get so discouraged. I go out and get drunk, and wake up with a throbbing headache. I promise myself I will never do it again. Sometimes I am able to do well for a week or even a couple of weeks, but then I fall again. I feel like such a failure. I have tried to hide it from my wife, but I can't even do that anymore. I have confessed it to the Lord a thousand times, but nothing seems to help. He has to be absolutely disgusted with me. There is one more thing that I just have to share with someone, and I can't share it with my wife. I can't even face God with it. I know you are going to think I'm a real scumbag.
>
> *Pastor:* Randy, I don't care what you share with me. It isn't going to make any difference how I see you. I know you are a child of God, and I love you like a brother.
>
> *Randy:* It's pornography! I got hooked on it a long time ago. I can't even look at a woman without thinking of sex. The temptation is overwhelming, and I can't seem to have any victory, no matter what I do. I don't want to live like this! It's ruining my marriage.
>
> *Pastor:* Randy, let's look at a passage of Scripture that seems to describe what you are experiencing. Romans 7:15 reads: "For that which I am doing, I do not understand; for I am not practicing what I would like to do, but I am doing the very thing I hate." Would you say that pretty well describes your life?
>
> *Randy:* Exactly! I really do desire to do what God says is right, and I hate being in bondage to alcohol and

lust. I don't know which one is worse. I get drunk
and wake up in some woman's bedroom. Or I sneak
down at night and click on the Internet. It is like I
step through a door and I can't turn around until
I'm drunk or I've masturbated—or worse. I don't
want to cheat on my wife. I know it's wrong, and I
feel disgusted with myself afterward.

Pastor: It sounds like you would identify with verse 16 as
well: "But if I do the very thing I do not wish to do, I
agree with the Law, confessing that it is good."
Randy, how many people are mentioned in this
verse?

Randy: There is only one person, and it is clearly "I."

Pastor: It is very defeating when we know what we want
to do, but for some reason we can't do it. How have
you tried to resolve this in your own mind?

> # SOMETIMES I WONDER IF I'M EVEN A CHRISTIAN. CHRISTIANITY SEEMS TO WORK FOR OTHERS BUT NOT FOR ME.

Randy: Sometimes I wonder if I'm even a Christian.
Christianity seems to work for others but not for me.
I sometimes question if the Christian life is even pos-
sible or if God is really here.

Pastor: You aren't alone, Randy. Many Christians believe
that they are different from others, and most think
they are the only ones who struggle with these

issues. If you were the only player in this battle, it would stand to reason that you would question your salvation or the existence of God. Let's take a look at verse 17: "So now, no longer am I the one doing it, but sin which indwells me." Now how many players are there?

Randy: Apparently two, but I don't understand.

Pastor: Let's read verse 18 and see if we can make some sense out of it: "For I know that nothing good dwells in me, that is, in my flesh; for the wishing is present in me, but the doing of the good is not."

Randy: I am familiar with that verse, because it describes me. I am no good for myself, and I'm no good for my wife. We would all be better off if I were dead.

Pastor: That's not true, because that is not what the verse says. In fact, it says the opposite. Something is dwelling in you, but it is not you. If I had a wood splinter in my finger, it would be "nothing good" dwelling in me. But the "nothing good" isn't me; it's the splinter. It is important to note that this "nothing good" is not even my flesh, but it is dwelling in my flesh.[1] If we see only ourselves in this struggle, it would be hopeless to live righteously. Paul was going to great lengths to tell us that there is a second party involved in our struggle, whose nature is evil and different from ours.

You see, Randy, when you and I were born, we lived under the penalty of sin, as every natural person does. We know that Satan and his emissaries are always working to keep us under that penalty. When God saved us, Satan lost that battle, but he didn't curl up his tail or pull in his fangs. His strategy now is to deceive us so that we continue to live under the power of sin. In 1 John 2:12-14, John identified little children of the faith as those who have been forgiven of their sins. In other words, they have overcome the penalty of sin. He identifies young men of the faith as those who have overcome the evil one. In other words, they have overcome the power of sin.

The passage we are looking at in Romans also says that this evil is going to work through the flesh, which remained with us after our salvation. It is our responsibility to crucify the flesh, and it is also our responsibility to resist the devil. Let's continue in the passage to see if we can learn more about how the battle is being waged: "For the good that I wish, I do not do; but I practice the very evil that I do not wish. But if I am doing the very thing I do not wish, I am no longer the one doing it, but sin which dwells in me. I find then the principle that evil is present in me, the one who wishes to do good" (vv. 19-21).

Randy: Sure, it is clearly evil and sin. But isn't it just my own sin? When I sin, I feel guilty.

Pastor: There is no question that you and I sin, but we are not sin as such. Evil is present in us, but we are not evil per se. This does not excuse us from sinning, because Paul wrote earlier, in Romans 6:12, that it is our responsibility not to let sin reign in our mortal body. The apostle John wrote in 1 John 1:8, "If we say that we have no sin, we are deceiving ourselves, and the truth is not in us." We must admit that we have sinned, but *having* sin and *being* sin are two totally different issues. When you come under conviction about your bondage to sin, what do you do?

Randy: I confess it to God.

Pastor: "Confession" literally means "to agree with God." It is the same thing as walking in the light or living in moral agreement with God about our present condition. We must do this if we are going to live in harmony with our heavenly Father, but it doesn't go far enough. Confession is the first step to repentance. The man that Paul was writing about agrees with God, acknowledging that what he is doing is wrong, but it doesn't resolve his problem. You have confessed your sin to God, but you are not experiencing victory over sin. That has to be very frustrating for you. The battle for your mind must be incredible. You probably entertain a lot of condemning thoughts as well as struggle with lustful thoughts. Have you ever felt so defeated that you just want to strike out at someone or at yourself?

> THAT IS PROBABLY WHY I GET DRUNK—
> TO DROWN OUT THOSE CONDEMNING,
> ACCUSING AND SOMETIMES
> BLASPHEMOUS THOUGHTS. I NEVER
> SEEM TO HAVE ANY MENTAL REST.

Randy: Almost every day! The battle for my mind is overwhelming. That is probably why I get drunk—to drown out those condemning, accusing and sometimes blasphemous thoughts. I never seem to have any mental rest.

Pastor: Do you ever entertain thoughts that are in line with who you really are as a child of God?

Randy: Sure, I know what is right and wrong. That is what makes it so hard. I know that what I am doing is wrong, and I hate it. I get this incredible desire for booze and sex. Then when I get my fill of them, I can't stand them. I hate them because of their hold on me. Then the next day I love them again. Or I should say, I lust after them again.

Pastor: Verse 22 explains why: "For I joyfully concur with the law of God in the inner man." When we act out of character with who we really are in Christ, the Holy Spirit immediately brings conviction, because of our union with God. Out of frustration and a sense of failure, we think or say things such as "I'm not going back to church anymore"; "Christianity doesn't work"; "It was God who made me this way"; "Now all I do is feel condemned"; "God promised to provide a way of escape. Well, where is it? I haven't found it!" At the same time, our true nature in the inner man begins to express itself: "I know what I'm doing is wrong, and I know the Bible says God loves me, but I am so frustrated by my continuing failure."

Randy: I always thought this passage was talking about a non-Christian.

Pastor: I know some good people who take that position, but that doesn't make sense to me. Does a natural man joyfully concur with the law of God in the inner man? Does an unbeliever agree with the law of God and confess that it is good? I don't think so! In fact, the non-Christian speaks out rather strongly against it. Some even hate Christians for upholding a moral standard. If you look carefully at this passage, you will notice that every disposition of his heart is directed toward God, and that cannot be said of a natural man. Mentally he knows what is right, the willingness is present, and he certainly feels like doing the right thing; but for some reason he can't. Now look at verse 23, which describes the nature of this battle with sin: "But I see a different law in the members of my body, waging war against the law of my mind, and making me a prisoner of the law of sin which is in my members." According to this passage, Randy, where is the battle being fought?

Randy: The battle appears to be in the mind.

Pastor: That is precisely where the battle is being fought. If Satan can get you to think you are the only one in the battle, you will get down on yourself or on God when you sin, which is counterproductive to resolving the problem. Let me put it this way: Suppose there is a closed door, which you are told not to open. There is a talking dog on the other side of the door, and the dog keeps saying, "Come on—let me in. You know you want to. Everyone is doing it. You will get away with it. Who would know?" You would probably open the door, even though you were told not to open it. Let's say the dog comes through the door and wraps his teeth around your leg. Would you beat on yourself or would you beat on the dog?

Randy: I would beat on the dog.

Pastor: Of course you would, and so would I. Before you open the door, the devil plays the role of tempter. When you open the door, he changes his strategy to accuser. Your mind is pounded with accusations: *You opened the door! You opened the door!* So you cry out, "God forgive me. I opened the door." Guess what

God does. He forgives you. Actually, you are already forgiven, but you confessed your sin, and that is good. But the dog is still there! You have submitted to God, but you haven't resisted the devil.

It is amazing what people will do to overcome their addictive behavior using their own strength and resources. Some try physical exercise; others take cold showers. The brave ones seek external accountability, while some isolate themselves like monks. Others take the path of self-destruction. I have seen young ladies purge themselves or take laxatives in order to defecate, for the same reason that others cut themselves. They are trying to purge themselves of evil. They sense that there is evil present in them, but the evil is not anything physical. Therefore, defecating, purging or cutting will not resolve it. Paul wrote, "These are matters which have, to be sure, the appearance of wisdom in self-made religion and self-abasement and severe treatment of the body, but are of no value against fleshly indulgence" (Col. 2:23). Many people get tired of beating on themselves, so they walk away from God under a cloud of defeat and condemnation. Paul expressed this feeling in verse 24 of Romans 7: "Wretched man that I am! Who will set me free from the body of this death?" He's not saying, "Wicked man that I am"; he's saying, "Miserable man that I am." All of his attempts to do the right thing meet with moral failure. There is nobody more miserable than someone who knows what is right and wants to do what is right but can't.

Randy: That's me. Miserable! And I don't see any way out of it. Death seems like the only option. Other times I just want to cut off my head to get rid of those voices.

Pastor: I have good news for you, Randy: There is victory. Jesus will set us free. Look at verse 25: "Thanks be to God through Jesus Christ our Lord! So then, on the one hand I myself with my mind am serving the law of God, but on the other, with my flesh the law of sin." Let's go back to the dog illustration. Why wasn't it enough just to cry out to God?

Randy: Well, like you said, the dog was still there. I guess I would have to chase the dog away.

Pastor: You would also have to close the door. You would have to cut off your sources of supply. If you have drug dealers who know your phone number, you need to change your phone number. If you have stashed a bottle at home for emergencies, you have to get rid of it. If you have a girlfriend on the side, you have to call her right now and tell her it is over.

Randy: I can't do that. I owe her something—at least an explanation. I will talk to her personally.

Pastor: You don't owe her anything. If you owe anybody, you owe your wife and children. As your pastor and friend, I am asking you to pick up that phone right now in my presence and tell her that it's over and that you never want to see her again. Then ask her forgiveness for involving her in adultery. If you don't, you will probably fall again.

Randy: I have told her several times that it's over, and I've confessed my sin so many times without any lasting change in my behavior.

Pastor: As you have already found out, that isn't enough. First, I want you to know that you are already forgiven. Christ died once for all your sins. He is not going to do it again. You were right in confessing your sins to God, because you do need to own up to the fact that you opened the door when you knew that it was wrong. Second, to make sure that every door is closed, you need to ask the Lord to reveal to your mind every unrighteous use of your body. That includes abusing your body with chemicals. As the Lord brings them to your mind, renounce every sexual use of your body that is immoral as well as every unrighteous use of your body that resulted in highs or drunkenness. Your body belongs to God, and it is not to be used in an unrighteous way. Then present your body to God as a living sacrifice, and reserve the sexual use of your body for your spouse only. Finally, resist the devil and he will flee from you.

Randy: I think I'm beginning to understand, but call to mind *every* unrighteous sexual use of my body? Listing them would take a long time! It might take a couple of hours, but I guess it would be a lot easier than living in bondage for the rest of my life. Would I have to renounce every time I got drunk? I've been condemning myself for my inability to live the Christian life, and I've been questioning my salvation. I see that Paul was frustrated about his failure, but he didn't get down on himself. He accepted his responsibility. More important, he expressed confidence by turning to God, because the Lord Jesus Christ would enable him to live above sin.

Pastor: You're on the right track. When you honestly ask the Lord to reveal every unrighteous use of your body, trust Him to bring to your mind what you need to renounce. He may or may not want you to recall every time you were drunk. He is the One who grants repentance. Condemning yourself won't help, because according to Romans 8:1 there is no condemnation for those who are in Christ Jesus. We don't want to assist the devil in his role as the accuser. Most people who are in bondage question their salvation. I have counseled hundreds who have shared with me their doubts about God and themselves. Ironically, the fact that they are sick about their sin and want to get out of it is one of the biggest assurances of their salvation. Randy, you have been trying to overcome sin in your own strength. You weren't created with that ability. God never instructed us to take on the devil. Oswald Chambers wrote, "Purity in God's children is not the outcome of obedience to His Law, but the result of the supernatural work of His grace. 'I will cleanse you'; 'I will give you a new heart'; 'I will put my Spirit within you and cause you to walk in My statutes'; 'I will do it all.'"[2]

Let me add just one note to this conversation. No one particular sin is isolated from the rest of reality. To experience your freedom in Christ and God's grace to overcome your sin, there are probably other issues that need to be resolved. With your permission, I would like to take you through the Steps to Freedom in Christ (see the epilogue) to resolve all your personal and spiritual conflicts. Then your repentance will be complete and the power of God will flow through you. You also need to understand the battle that is going on for your mind, and that is what I will deal with in the next chapter.

GOING DEEPER

1. In what ways do you identify with Randy?
2. What parts of the pastor's advice can you apply to your life?
3. Have you ever wondered if you are a Christian? Why? How does the pastor's response to Randy on this matter speak to you?
4. Have you confessed your sins many times but have seen very few results or changes? How does the pastor's response to Randy apply to you?

Notes

1. The *New International Version* of the Bible translates *sarx* (flesh) as the sinful, or old, nature. In all translations, the "nothing good" is not the flesh or the sinful nature; rather, the "nothing good" is operating in the sinful nature.
2. Oswald Chambers, *God's Workmanship* (Fort Washington, PA: Christian Literature Crusade, 1960), p. 75.

CHAPTER 8

HOW MENTAL
STRONGHOLDS
ARE FORMED

*If we let ourselves believe that man began with divine grace, that he
forfeited this by sin, and that he can be redeemed only by divine grace
through the crucified Christ, then we shall find a peace of mind never
granted to philosophers. He who cannot believe is cursed, for he reveals
by his belief that God has not chosen to give him grace.*

BLAISE PASCAL

*Life is a hard fight, a struggle, a wrestling with the principle of evil, hand to
hand, foot to foot. Every inch of the way must be disputed. The night is given us to
take breath, to pray, to drink deep at the fountain of power. The day, to use the
strength which has been given to us, to go forth to work with it till the evening.*

FLORENCE NIGHTINGALE

If you are currently struggling with habitual sins, how do you respond to the following biblical truths:

- The old self (man) is dead, and the new self (man) is alive.
- We've been transferred out of the kingdom of darkness and into the kingdom of God's beloved Son.
- We are no longer "in Adam"; we are presently "in Christ."
- We are no longer children of wrath; rather, we are now children of God.
- We are alive to Christ and dead to sin.
- We are no longer bond servants of sin; rather, we are bond servants of Christ.

As Christians, we all want to believe what the Bible clearly teaches, but many find themselves wondering, *If that is true, then how come I don't feel very different from how I felt before I received Christ?* or, *Why am I still struggling with the same issues I struggled with before I became a Christian?*

REPROGRAMMING OUR MINDS

Let me explain why believers continue to struggle with many of the same cravings, thoughts and feelings that they struggled with before they believed. I have already written about the bigger picture, but let's do a quick review. Because of the Fall, we were all born physically alive but spiritually dead in our trespasses and sins (see Eph. 2:1). We had neither the presence of God in our lives nor the knowledge of His ways. Therefore, during our early formative years, we learned how to live our lives independently of God. We had no choice. Then one day we heard the gospel and decided to invite Jesus into our lives. We were born again. We became new creations in Christ, but everything that had previously been programmed into our memory banks was still there. Nobody pushed the delete button! That is why Paul wrote,

> Do not conform any longer to the pattern of this world, but be transformed by the renewing of your mind. Then you will be able to test and approve what God's will is— his good, pleasing and perfect will (Rom. 12:2, *NIV*).

When we have been truly born again, we are both physically and spiritually alive. A greater transformation took place when we were born again spiritually than will take place when we die physically. When we die physically, we will be absent from our body and present with the Lord. Until then, we have to do something with our physical body, which is what the last two chapters have been about. Recall that Paul urged us to present our body to God as a living sacrifice and not to use our body as an instrument of unrighteousness. That truth is summarized in Romans 12:1. The next verse declares that we must reprogram our mind, because it was previously programmed to live independently of God. These are the two most critical issues that confront us as believers: doing something about the neutral disposition of our physical body and reprogramming our mind to the truth of God's Word.

When I was in the United States Navy, it was customary to refer to the captain of our ship as the old man. The first captain I had was a lousy old man. He belittled his officers and drank excessively with the senior enlisted men. If I was going to survive on board that ship, I had to learn how to cope and how to defend myself under his authority. One day he got transferred to another post. He was gone forever, and I no longer had any relationship with him. I was no longer under his authority. We got a new old man, and he was a good one. But how do you think I continued to live on board that ship? I lived the way I had been trained under the former old man. Slowly I began to realize that my old means of coping were no longer necessary. I had to learn a new way to live under the authority of my new captain.

This analogy applies to our spiritual lives. We are no longer under the authority of the god of this world, because our relationship with him has been severed. We are children of the true God. Our greatest priority is to get to know this new captain of our soul. That's why Paul wrote, "I consider everything a loss compared to the surpassing greatness of knowing Christ Jesus my Lord" (Phil. 3:8, *NIV*).

UNDERSTANDING HOW STRONGHOLDS DEVELOP

Like computers, our brain has recorded every experience we have ever had. These impressions have an impact on our physical body. I have seen adults recoil in physical pain as they reconnect with childhood memories of abuse. This happens because strongholds against the knowledge of God were raised up in their mind. These strongholds have affected our temperament. It will take time to renew our mind and to replace the lies we have believed with the truth of God's Word. The fact that we have all the resources that we need to do this is the good news (gospel). The Lord has sent the Holy Spirit, who is the Spirit of truth (see John 14:16-17), to guide us into all truth (see John 16:13). Because we are one with God, "We have the mind of Christ" (1 Cor. 2:16). We have superior weapons to win the battle for our mind, according to Paul, who in 2 Corinthians 10:3-5 (*NIV*) wrote,

> For though we live in the world, we do not wage war as the world does. The weapons we fight with are not the weapons of the world. On the contrary, they have divine

power to demolish strongholds. We demolish arguments and every pretension that sets itself up against the knowledge of God, and we take captive every thought to make it obedient to Christ.

Paul was not referring to defensive armor; he was referring to battering-ram weaponry that tears down strongholds that have been raised up against the knowledge of God.

How are these strongholds erected in our mind? There is general agreement among developmental theorists that our attitudes are primarily assimilated from the environment in which we are raised. The primary programming of our mind took place in early childhood in two ways. First, it took place through prevailing experiences such as the families in which we were raised, the churches which we did or didn't attend, the neighborhoods in which we grew up, the communities to which we belonged, the friends that we had or didn't have and other similar influences upon our lives. Each aspect had an effect upon the development of our mind and contributed to our worldview.

In addition to prevailing experiences, another major contributor to our development of mental strongholds was traumatic experiences. For instance, we may have been raped as a child, our mom and dad could have divorced, or somebody close to us could have died. These experiences were not assimilated into our mind over time; rather, they were burned into our mind due to their intensity. All of these experiences were filed away in our memory, and we have no delete button in our organic computer.

However, the environment was not the only factor in our development. Two children can be raised in the same home, have the same parents, eat the same food, have similar friends and go to the same church, yet they respond differently and, as a result, see the world differently. Another significant factor is God: He has known us from the foundation of the world (see Eph. 2:10) and created us uniquely in our mother's womb. Jacob and Esau came from the same womb, but they were very different people.

As we struggle to reprogram our mind, we are also confronted daily with a world system that is not godly. Remember, Paul warned us, "Do not conform *any longer* to the pattern of this world" (Rom. 12:2, *NIV*, emphasis added). We can continue, even as Christians, to allow the world in which we live to affect our mind. That is why Paul warned, "See to it that no one takes you captive through hollow and deceptive philosophy, which depends on human tradition and the basic principles of this world rather than on Christ" (Col. 2:8, *NIV*).

STANDING AGAINST TEMPTATION

Since we live in this world, we are going to continuously face the reality of temptation. It's not a sin to be tempted. If that were the case, then the worst sinner who ever lived would be Jesus, because He "has been tempted in every way, just as we are—yet

> IT'S NOT A SIN TO BE TEMPTED. IF THAT WERE THE CASE, THEN THE WORST SINNER WHO EVER LIVED WOULD BE JESUS.

was without sin" (Heb. 4:15, *NIV*). Satan knows exactly which buttons to push in each of us. He knows our weaknesses and our family histories. Things that tempt one of us may not tempt another. For instance, when was the last time you were tempted to turn a rock into bread? That temptation was unique to Christ.

It was an attempt by Satan to get Jesus to use His divine attributes independently of the Father to save Himself. He faced the temptation by quoting a passage from the book of Deuteronomy: "It is written: 'Man does not live by bread alone, but on every word that comes from the mouth of God'" (Matt. 4:4, *NIV*). Every temptation is an attempt by Satan to get us to live our lives independently of God, to walk according to the flesh rather than according to the Spirit (see Gal. 5:16-23).

We cannot, nor should we try to, fully isolate ourselves from this world, so we must learn how to stand against temptation. Temptation begins with a seed thought in our mind. Alcohol is socially acceptable, sex is used to sell everything from beer to cars, and gambling is sanctioned by the state. As a result, we are going to be constantly bombarded. However, those who struggle with sexual sins don't need temptations from the external world to spark another episode of sin—there is so much junk programmed into their memory bank that they could fantasize for years without ever leaving their homes. That is why sexual strongholds are so difficult. Once they are formulated in the mind, the mental impressions are readily available for recall.

If we are going to take the way of escape that God has provided for us, we must take the original thought captive to the obedience of Christ. If we allow tempting thoughts to ruminate in our mind, we will eventually take a path that leads to destruction. For instance, suppose a man is struggling with addictions to alcohol and pornography. One night his wife asks him to go to the store for some milk. As he gets into his car, for a brief moment he wrestles in his mind as to which store he should go to. He decides upon a local deli that also sells liquor and pornography. He didn't have to go to that store. He could have gotten milk at a grocery store where the atmosphere is more wholesome. The moment he steers his car toward the deli, the battle for his mind has been lost. Before he reaches the store, rationalizing thoughts cross his mind: *If you don't want me to buy any booze, Lord, have my pastor be at the store buying milk. If you don't want me to look at any pornography, Lord, let my mother call me on my cell phone before I get to the store.* Since no pastor or anyone else he knows is present, he buys the booze. Since his cell phone does not ring, he takes a peek at just a couple of the dirty magazines.

The undisciplined mind can momentarily rationalize, but the relief doesn't last. Before the man in this illustration has even left the store, guilt and shame overwhelm him. The tempter has now become the accuser: *You sick person, when are you going to get over this? How can you call yourself a Christian?* On his drive home he cries out, "Lord, forgive me. I will never do it again." Until tomorrow!

This man needed to make the choice to take the way of escape *before* he got into his car. Rare is the person who can turn the car around once the plan has been set in motion. Why is that?

CORRELATING THE OUTER PERSON WITH THE INNER PERSON

To answer that question, please refer to figure 2. Scripture teaches that we have an outer person and an inner person (see 2 Cor. 4:16). The outer person is our physical body, which relates to the world. Our brain is a part of the outer person. Our mind is a part of the inner person. There is a fundamental difference between our brain and our mind. Our brain is organic! When we physically die, it will return to dust. We will be absent from the body, but we will not be mindless.

It only makes sense that God created the outer person to correlate with the inner person. The correlation between the mind and the brain is obvious. The brain functions much like a digital computer. Every neuron operates like a little switch that turns on and off. Each has many inputs (dendrites) and only one

Figure 2

output that channels the neurotransmitters to other dendrites. Billions of these brain cells make up the computer hardware. The mind, on the other hand, has a role similar to the software of a computer. The brain cannot function any other way than how it has been programmed. The brain receives external data, and the mind interprets it.

People in the Western world have a tendency to assume that mental problems are primarily caused by faulty hardware. There is no question that organic brain syndrome, Alzheimer's disease or some lesser organic problem such as a chemical imbalance can impede our ability to function. The best program won't work if the computer is turned off or in disrepair. However, I think that the primary problem is not the hardware; it's the software. We can do little to fix the hardware, but we can change the software. Now that we are alive in Christ, we have the mind of Christ at the core of our being.

The Peripheral Nervous System and Our Will

The brain and the spinal cord make up the central nervous system, which branches off into the peripheral nervous system. The peripheral nervous system has two channels: somatic and auto-nomic. The somatic nervous system regulates our muscular and skeletal movements—such as speech and gestures—over which we have volitional control. The somatic nervous system corre-lates with the will.

Our autonomic nervous system regulates our glands. We have no volitional control over our glands. We don't say to our heart, "Beat, beat, beat"; or to our adrenal glands, "Adren, adren, adren"; or to our thyroid, "Thy, thy, thy." They function auto-matically.

Sex glands are part of the autonomic nervous system. For instance, a woman has no volitional control over her menstrual cycle. A man can wake up in the middle of the night with an erec-tion, and it may have nothing to do with lust. It is just part of a rhythmic cycle that all men go through about every 90 minutes. That is the way God created us.

If we have no control over our sex glands, then how can God expect us to have any sexual self-control? The good news is, we don't need to have any volitional control of our sex glands in order to have self-control. We need to take control of what we think. Our sex glands are not the cause of sexual immorality. They will naturally function in their God-given way. However, if we load the brain up with pornography, our autonomic nervous system will simply respond. We may not have any control over what comes out, but we do have control over what we put in. Just like a computer: garbage in, garbage out!

We can choose which movies we see and which magazines we read, but we can't totally isolate ourselves from the filth in this world. Christians may have to work in an atmosphere saturated with pinups and other sexually explicit material. Businessmen who are on the wagon still need to attend luncheon appoint-ments where alcohol is served. What we see in the world comes through the gateway of our eyes. We could stop the flow by closing our eyes, but even then our imaginations could run wild. If we look at some object of temptation, the signal will be recorded in our brains. At that moment, we have a choice. If we choose to let our mind dwell on it, there will be an immediate physiological response, because the peripheral nervous system is fed by the central nervous system.

Have you ever wondered why it is so hard to remember some things yet so easy to recall others? When I was a seminary student, I would spend half the night studying Greek and then pray that the "register" didn't clear before I took the exam. It was a struggle to remember. Pornography was different. If I saw one image, it seemed to stay in my mind for years. Why is that? Part of the answer is physical. When we are sexually stimulated, a signal is sent to our glands, which secrete hormones into the bloodstream. The more emotionally excited we are, the greater the release of hormones. They pass through the brain and lock in whatever visual or audio stimulus is present at the time of the emotional excitement. It causes us to involuntarily remember traumatic events as well as emotionally positive ones. Pleasant memories enhance learning and stay with us longer. I wish I could have gotten more emotionally excited about Greek!

People can become emotionally excited and sexually stimulated by just entertaining thoughts of sexual activity. That is why people will have an emotional rush before there is even any physical contact. The man going to the store where pornography is sold will be sexually stimulated long before he sees the magazines. The thinking has caused the rush. It started with his thoughts, which triggered his nervous system, which responded by secreting hormones into the bloodstream.

Alcoholics have the same problem. They can have an adrenaline rush before they take their first drink. They will start licking their lips when they see a bottle of booze or an advertisement on television. That is why the government has limited hard-liquor and tobacco advertising on television. If addicts let their minds go down that path, they will have all kinds of physiological and emotional responses within minutes or seconds. Just thinking about it can cause their mouth to water and palms to sweat.

The Autonomic Nervous System and Our Emotions

Our autonomic nervous system obviously correlates to the emotional part of our inner being. Just as we can't control our glands, we can't directly control our emotions. If you think you can, give it a try! Try liking someone right now that you previously couldn't stand. We can't order our emotions that way. However, we must acknowledge our emotions, because we can't be right with God and not be real. We do have control over what we think, and that is the basis for self-control: "Brothers, stop thinking like children. In regard to evil be infants, but in your thinking be adults" (1 Cor. 14:20, *NIV*).

> DROP THE FOLLOWING LINE FROM YOUR VOCABULARY, WHETHER IT IS IN REFERENCE TO YOURSELF OR OTHERS: "YOU SHOULDN'T FEEL THAT WAY." IT'S A SUBTLE FORM OF REJECTION, AND NO ADDICT NEEDS ANY MORE OF THAT.

The concept of "adults only" is a travesty. It implies that there is one standard of morality for adults and another for children. Pornography is wrong at any age. If it is wrong for a child to drink alcohol, why is it right for adults? At what age does it become right? Adults should have a greater degree of self-control, but how do they develop self-control? How many adults have mastery over sin without Christ? Mature adults should know enough to stay away from pornography and not allow their mind to be programmed with filth. The law requires television programmers to announce, "The content of the following movie is suitable for mature audiences only. Viewer discretion is advised." Pornography isn't suitable for anyone, and mature people should be the first to know that. Once images are put in the mind, they are going to stay there.

Since we have no control over how we feel, I encourage you to drop the following line from your vocabulary, whether it is in reference to yourself or others: "You shouldn't feel that way." It's a subtle form of rejection, and no addict needs any more of that. What can we do about how we feel? Nothing! The real issue is what we believe about God, ourselves and the environment around us. Perhaps people who feel a particular way have not fully understood the whole situation, maybe they have wrongly judged someone or maybe they just need to trust God.

Our feelings are primarily a product of our thought lives. The tendency is to believe that something or somebody has made us feel a certain way, but that really isn't true. All external data is processed by our mind, which we have control over. It would logically follow that our feelings can be distorted by what we choose to believe. If what we choose to believe does not reflect truth, then what we feel will not reflect reality.

Suppose your company is downsizing and you have seen some of your colleagues let go. On Monday morning you find a note on your desk from your boss requesting that you see him on Friday at 10:00 A.M. Can you imagine all the emotions you will go through that week? At first you may be angry, because you believe you are going to be laid off. If you don't know for sure what your boss is going to say or do, you may feel anxious. By the middle of the week, you may be convinced in your own mind that you are getting the axe on Friday. Since you don't have any options for other work, you are depressed. Friday morning arrives and you are a basket case emotionally. As you walk, all depressed and anxious, into your boss's office, he says, "Congratulations! I have just promoted you to vice president." With that, you faint on the spot. All the emotions you felt that week did not conform to reality, because what you were thinking wasn't based on truth.

IDENTIFYING THE CAUSES OF SEVERAL STRONGHOLDS

We all face temptations on a daily basis. The devil wants us to live according to the flesh and therefore independently of God. Suppose we consciously make a choice to give in to the temptation. If we continue to act upon that choice, we will establish a habit in about six weeks. If the habit persists, a stronghold will be developed in our mind.

A stronghold is a habitual pattern of thought, or memory traces, burned into our mind over time or by the intensity of traumatic experiences. It is like driving a truck through a pasture over and over again. Before long, deep ruts are made in the moist soil, and the truck will naturally stay in those ruts. In fact, any effort made to steer out of those ruts will be met with resistance. Author and speaker Ed Silvoso defines a stronghold as "a mind-set impregnated with hopelessness that causes us to accept as unchangeable, situations that we know are contrary to the will of God."[1] Mental strongholds are similar to what some call flesh patterns and what psychologists call defense mechanisms. There are an infinite number of potential combinations that can make up strongholds.

Most Christians struggle with feelings of inferiority. Inferiority complexes are not formed overnight; rather, they happen to people who were raised in a performance-based system—which is the case for almost everybody. No matter how hard we try, we will never be able to live up to someone else's expectations. We strive for that elusive acceptance that never comes because we never measure up. Being raised according to this world's system, we inevitably struggle with some sense of inferiority, because there will always be somebody who is stronger, smarter or prettier.

> INFERIORITY COMPLEXES ARE NOT FORMED OVERNIGHT; RATHER, THEY HAPPEN TO PEOPLE WHO WERE RAISED IN A PERFORMANCE-BASED SYSTEM— WHICH IS THE CASE FOR ALMOST EVERYBODY.

People who have been raised in alcoholic homes will have mental strongholds. Let's use three boys as an example. For this illustration let's say they were raised by a father who after years of drinking became addicted. The older boy believed that he was strong enough to stand up to Dad. There was no way he was going to take anything from this drunk. The second boy didn't believe he could stand up to Dad, so he would accommodate him. The youngest boy was terrorized. When their father would come home, the boy headed for the closet or hid under the bed. Twenty years later, the father is gone. These three boys are now adults. When they are confronted with a hostile situation, how do they respond? The older one will fight, the middle one will accommodate, and the younger one will run and hide.

Homosexuality is another stronghold, probably one of the most resistant to conventional treatment. Those who are caught in the web of this stronghold weren't born that way. They may have been genetically predisposed with certain strengths and weaknesses, but that predisposition did not make them homosexual. Homosexuality is a lie, another false identity with which we label ourselves or others. There is no such thing as a homosexual. God created us male and female. There are homosexual thoughts, feelings and behaviors—and the latter is what the Lord condemns. Heaping condemnation upon those who struggle with homosexuality will prove counterproductive. They don't need any more condemnation. They suffer from an incredible identity crisis already. Overbearing authoritarianism is what drove many of them to that lifestyle in the first place.

Most people who struggle with homosexual tendencies or behaviors have had poor developmental upbringing. Sexual abuse, dysfunctional families in which the parental roles are reversed, exposure to homosexual literature before having the opportunity to fully develop their own sexual identity, playground teasing and poor relationships with members of the opposite sex—these all contribute to the mental and emotional development of those who struggle with homosexuality. The events that precipitated these mental and emotional difficulties have to be resolved, and the mind has to be reprogrammed with the truth of God's Word.

Sometimes it is difficult to find a precipitating event. How then do we explain how this stronghold developed? Suppose a young man looks at another naked man in a locker room at school and has a tempting thought. That is all it is, just a tempting thought, and he may dismiss it the first time. Then it happens again and again, so he begins to think, *Why am I thinking these thoughts? If I am thinking these thoughts, then maybe I am one of them.* The sexual stronghold becomes entrenched the moment he believes that lie. Instead of taking every thought captive to the obedience of Christ, he lets his mind dwell on sexual thoughts and that affects his feelings. Then he physically involves himself with another man, and sin begins to reign in his mortal body because he has used his body as an instrument of unrighteousness.

To overcome the sin that wages war in our members, we have to renounce the unrighteous use of our body, submit it to God as a living sacrifice and be transformed by the renewing of our mind. However, we still do not have the complete answer. The enemies of our sanctification are the world, the flesh *and* the devil. In the next chapter we will discuss the spiritual battle for our mind; then we will have all the tools we need to tear down mental strongholds.

GOING DEEPER

1. Why is it important to identify and deal with strongholds that affect our lives?
2. What does having "the mind of Christ" mean?
3. What is the difference between the outer person and the inner person? How do they work together?
4. How do our choices in life affect the outer person and the inner person?

Note

1. Ed Silvoso, *That None Should Perish* (Ventura, CA: Regal Books, 1994), p. 155.

CHAPTER 9

TEARING DOWN STRONGHOLDS

The sins of the mind are the last habitation of the devil.

JAROL JOHNSON

When God wants us to move a mountain, he does not take a bar of iron,
but he takes a little worm. The fact is, we have too much strength.
We are not weak enough. It is not our strength that we want. One drop of
God's strength is worth more than all the world.

DWIGHT L. MOODY

A struggling addict said, "I guess I'm not strong enough."

Mike responded, "That is not your problem. The problem is you are too strong. As long as you think you can get out of this by your own strength and resources, you will continue trying. You are trying to save your pride, and that is keeping you from experiencing the grace of God."

Many of us try to overcome slavery to sin on our own. Some of us put our confidence in secular programs and popular strategies. These may help addicts achieve a degree of abstinence, but the emotional, mental and spiritual freedom for which they long will continue to elude them. We cannot achieve total control of our lives by sheer human effort.

Ironically, when we surrender to the lordship of Christ, we experience self-control, which is a fruit of the Spirit. We are saved and sanctified by faith, not by how we behave. Paul wrote,

> Not that we are adequate in ourselves to consider anything as coming from ourselves, but our adequacy is from God, who also made us adequate as servants of a new covenant, not of the letter, but of the Spirit; for the letter kills, but the Spirit gives life (2 Cor. 3:5-6).

The Holy Spirit gives us life, strength and direction, but there are counterfeit spirits that will lead us astray and keep us in bondage. A pastor shared with me that a number of people in his church were chemically dependent. In response, they had plans to start a ministry to help people who wanted to overcome their addictions. They all insisted that the catch phrase on the front of their brochure read "Are you tired of listening to those voices?" What are those voices, and how can we win this battle for our mind? Winning this battle is the last piece in the recovery puzzle.

RECEIVING MIXED MESSAGES

There are all kinds of mixed messages in this world. Consequently, there are a lot of mixed emotions. Some Christians don't feel saved, don't feel like God loves them, don't believe they're worth anything. These messages aren't true, but many of us believe them, which results in irresponsible behavior and troubled emotions. Scripture clearly teaches that all the messages we receive aren't necessarily from the world. Paul wrote, "The Spirit clearly says that in later times some will abandon the faith and follow deceiving spirits and things taught by demons" (1 Tim. 4:1, *NIV*). I have counseled hundreds of people who were hearing voices or struggling with tempting, accusing and blasphemous thoughts. In many cases, it has proven to be a spiritual battle for their mind.

If Satan can get us to believe a lie, he will keep us in bondage emotionally, mentally and spiritually; and as a result we will give up some degree of control in our lives. His primary strategy is to distort the truth about our identity and position in Christ, and distort our understanding of God. I have talked with seminary students who intellectually know that God is omnipresent, omnipotent, omniscient, kind and loving in all His ways; but when asked about their feelings toward God, many respond, "I'm not sure He loves me!" Their feelings don't conform to reality, because thoughts have been raised up against the knowledge of God. Satan can't do anything about our position in Christ, but if he can get us to believe it isn't true, we will live as though it's not. People don't always live according to what they profess, but they always live according to what they believe.

Our problems don't just stem from what we believed in the past. Paul said we must continuously take every thought captive to the obedience of Christ (see 2 Cor. 10:5). The word "thought" comes from the Greek word *noema*. Notice how else Paul used this word in the same epistle: "I have forgiven in the sight of Christ for your sake, in order that Satan might not outwit us. For we are not unaware of his schemes [noema]" (2:10-11, *NIV*). I believe the greatest access that Satan has to the Church is our unwillingness to forgive those who have offended us. It certainly has been true with the thousands that we have had the privilege to work with.

In another passage, Paul wrote, "The god of this age has blinded the minds [noema] of unbelievers, so that they cannot see the light of the gospel of the glory of Christ" (2 Cor. 4:4, *NIV*). Think of the implications that this has for world evangelization. Let's consider one more passage from this epistle: "I am afraid that just as Eve was deceived by the serpent's cunning, your minds [noema] may somehow be led astray from your sincere and pure devotion to Christ" (11:3, *NIV*). I'm concerned, too.

RECOGNIZING THE SPIRITUAL BATTLE

Attend almost any recovery meeting and the leaders will advise addicts not to pay attention to that committee in their heads. What is that committee? Counselors refer to this battle for the mind as stinking thinking, which is a given for those who struggle with addictive behaviors. Solomon said in reference to those who drink too much, "Your eyes will see strange things, and your mind will utter perverse things" (Prov. 23:33). This is nothing more than a struggle with our old nature (flesh), or is it?

If there is a spiritual battle going on for our mind, why don't we recognize it? For one reason: I can't read your mind, and you can't read mine. We really don't have any idea what is going on in the minds of other people unless they have the courage to share that with us. In many cases they won't, because in our culture they fear that others will assume they are mentally ill. Clients will talk about their abuse or what has happened to them in the past, but only to the right person would they dare share what is going on inside their head. Are they mentally ill, or is a battle being waged for control of their mind? The lack of any balanced biblical contribution to mental health professions has left them with only one conclusion: Any problem in the mind must either be psychological or neurological.

People who have panic attacks, suffer from severe depression or see things that no one else sees will likely be diagnosed as having chemical imbalances. They will probably be given a prescription for medication with the hope of curing the problem or eliminating the symptoms. Other sufferers self-medicate with alcohol or drugs. Our body chemistry can get out of balance and cause mental and emotional discomfort. Hormonal problems can throw off our systems, but other legitimate questions need to be asked: How can a chemical produce a personal thought? How can our neurotransmitters involuntarily and randomly fire in such a way that they create thoughts that we are opposed to thinking? Is there a natural explanation for that? I'm willing to hear any legitimate answers and explanations, because I care for people and I don't want them to live defeated lives. I also want to see their problems resolved by the grace of God, but I don't think that will happen in many cases unless we take into account the reality of the spiritual world.

WHEN PEOPLE SAY THEY ARE HEARING VOICES, WHAT ARE THEY ACTUALLY HEARING?

When people say they are hearing voices, what are they actually hearing? The only way that we can physically hear with our ears is to have a sound source that compresses air molecules. Sound waves move through the physical medium of air and strike our eardrums, which send a signal to our brain. That is how we physically hear. The voices that people hear, or the thoughts with which some struggle, are not coming from that kind of source.

In a similar way, when people say they see things that others don't see, what are they actually seeing? The only way that we can naturally see something is to have a light source reflecting off a material object to our eyes, which sends a signal to our brain. Satan and his demons are spiritual beings; they do not have material substance, so we cannot see or hear a spiritual being with our natural eyes and ears.

> For our struggle is not against flesh and blood, but against rulers, against the authorities, against the powers of this dark world and against the spiritual forces of evil in the heavenly realms (Eph. 6:12, *NIV*).

The battle is in the mind, because there is not a physical presence that can reflect light rays and originate physical sound. The secular world knows nothing of the spiritual world, so people who do not believe in God have no choice but to consider some natural explanation for what is being reported to them. Let me illustrate with the following e-mail that I received:

> For years I had those "voices" in my head. There were four in particular and sometimes what seemed like loud choruses of them. When the subject of schizophrenia would come up on television or in a magazine, I would think to myself, *I know I am not schizophrenic, but what is this in my head?* I was tortured, mocked and jeered—every single thought I had was second-guessed—consequently, I had zero self-esteem. I often used to wish the voices would be quiet, and I always wondered if other people had this as well and if it was common.

When I started to learn from you about taking every thought captive to Christ and read about other people's experiences with these voices, I came to recognize them for what they were, and I was able to make them leave.

That was an amazing and beautiful thing, to be fully quiet in my mind after so many years of torment. I do not need to explain further all the wonderful things that come with this freedom of the mind; it is a blessing you seem to know well.[1]

RESISTING THE ENEMY

The answer is not to cast out a demon of homosexuality, a demon of lust or a demon of alcoholism. That kind of simplistic thinking has damaged the credibility of the Church and left the addict without a complete answer. I have seen Christianity mocked on primetime television by a parade of homosexuals and lesbians who have left the Church because well-meaning Christians had tried to cast out of them a demon of this or a demon of that. Don't get me wrong. There is no question that Satan is part of the problem, and his demons do tempt, accuse and deceive us if we let them. They will take advantage of any ground that we give to them.

Simply casting a demon out of someone doesn't take into consideration all the other dimensions of reality, and I personally don't think that it is the best method for resolving spiritual conflicts. Defeated Christians are like a house filled with garbage—the trash hasn't been taken out in months and things have been spilled without being cleaned up. It attracts a lot of flies. We can study the flight pattern of all the flies, determine who their commander in chief is and get the name and rank of every fly, but that will not resolve the problem. Even if we manage to chase them off, they will come right back. We have to get rid of the garbage. Repentance and faith in God has been and will continue to be the answer. We do this by submitting to God and resisting the devil (see Jas. 4:7). If we try to resist the devil without first submitting to God, we will have a dogfight. We can submit to God and not resist the devil, but we will stay in bondage. It is a tragedy that most recovery programs aren't doing either one.

Paul admonished us to put on the armor of God (see Eph. 6:10-18). The belt of truth defends us against the father of lies. The breastplate of righteousness is our protection against the accuser of the brethren. Then Paul summarized by saying, "In addition to all, tak[e] up the shield of faith with which you will be able to extinguish all the flaming missiles of the evil one" (Eph. 6:16). The "flaming missiles" are just tempting, accusing and deceptive thoughts that everybody has to deal with. Healthy Christians don't pay attention to them. We know the truth and we choose to believe it. What happens if we don't take every thought captive to the obedience of Christ? If we entertain such thoughts, we will develop strongholds in the mind, lustful habits and emotional attachments.

Don't assume that all disturbing thoughts are from Satan. Whether a thought came from the television set, the memory bank, the pit or the imagination doesn't matter in one sense, because the answer is the same. We have to choose to think the truth. We could try to analyze the source of every thought, but that wouldn't resolve the problem. We would only be caught up in our own subjective maze. Too much time is spent in the paralysis of analysis. Providing a brilliant analysis of addictive behaviors and telling people why they suffer from those addictions don't solve the problem.

FINDING HOPE FOR OUR FREEDOM

In order for people to find their freedom in Christ, they must assume responsibility for their own attitudes and actions. We can't forgive for them, renounce for them or think for them. It is every individual's responsibility to submit to God and to resist the devil. The role of the pastor or counselor is explained in 2 Timothy 2:24-26 (*NIV*):

> The Lord's servant must not quarrel; instead, he must be kind to everyone, able to teach, not resentful. Those who oppose him he must gently instruct, in the hope that God will grant them repentance leading to a knowledge of the truth, and that they will come to their senses and escape from the trap of the devil, who has taken them captive to do his will.

This is not a power model; it is a kind, patient and able-to-teach model. It clearly shows that the Lord is the One who grants repentance and sets us free. It also reveals that the battle is in the mind, and that is why truth sets the captives free—provided the people under bondage know the truth and choose to believe it.

Can we tear down mental strongholds? Yes, we can. If we have been trained in the wrong way, we can be retrained. If our mind has been programmed wrongly, it can be reprogrammed. If we learned something the wrong way, we can learn to do it the right way. If we believed a lie, we can decide to renounce the lie and choose to believe the truth. However, it will take the rest of our lives to renew our mind and mature in Christ. Our mind will never be fully renewed, and our character will always fall short of perfection, but that is still our pursuit. The growth process will be stopped, however, if we have not resolved our personal and spiritual conflicts through genuine repentance and faith in God. Those living in bondage go from book to book, program to program, pastor to pastor and counselor to counselor; but nothing seems to work. They can't grow, because they are chained to the past. They have unresolved issues between themselves and God, which are keeping them from experiencing His grace; and they are being distracted and deceived by the father of lies.

When I was a young Christian, I decided to clean up my mind. When I made that decision, did the battle get easier or harder? It got harder, of course. Temptation isn't much of a battle if we easily give in to it. It is fierce when we decide to stand against it. I didn't become a Christian until I was in my 20s, even though I had gone to church all of my life. I had a good moral upbringing, for which I am thankful; but after spending four years in the United States Navy, my mind had been exposed to a lot of junk. I didn't drink during my first two years in the military. Then I started to join my friends. Fortunately, I didn't drink long enough or often enough to establish a habit, but I had seen a lot of pornography, which was a problem. After one look, images would dance in my mind for months and years. I hated it. I struggled every time I went to a place where pornography was available. I finally got the victory. Let me share how.

Think of the mind as a coffeepot. We desire the water inside to be pure, but unfortunately, we have added some coffee grounds. There is no way to filter out the coffee once it has been added, so the water inside is dark and polluted. Sitting beside the coffeepot is a huge bowl of crystal-clear ice, which represents the Word of God. We are only able to put in one or two cubes a day, so it may seem a little futile at first. But over the course of time, the water begins to look less polluted, and we can hardly taste or smell the presence of the coffee. The process works, provided we stop adding more coffee grounds.

For most people, this process of winning the battle for their mind will initially be two steps forward and one step back. With persistence it becomes three steps forward and one back, and then four and five steps forward, as we learn to take every thought captive in obedience to Christ. We may despair with all the steps back, but God isn't going to give up on us.

Remember, our sins are already forgiven. We only need to keep living by faith and taking every thought captive in obedience to Christ. That means we don't think on anything but that which is true. This is a winnable war since we are already alive in Christ and dead to sin. Christ has already won the greater battle. Freedom to be all God has called us to be is the greatest blessing in this present life. This freedom is worth the fight. As we learn more about who we are as children of God and the nature of the battle for our mind, the process gets easier. Eventually it will be 20 steps forward and one back, and finally the steps are all forward with only an occasional slip in the battle for the mind.

Paul wrote, "Let the peace of Christ rule in your hearts, since as members of one body you were called to peace. And be thankful" (Col. 3:15, *NIV*). How we do that is explained in the next verse: "Let the word of Christ dwell in you richly" (*NIV*). We have to fill our mind with the crystal-clear Word of God; there is no alternative plan. Just trying to stop thinking bad thoughts won't

> # WE OVERCOME THE FATHER OF LIES BY CHOOSING THE TRUTH!

work. Rebuking all those tempting, accusing and deceiving thoughts will not work. We are only treading water if that is what we're doing, and we will make no progress toward recovery. We would be like a person in the middle of a lake who is treading water and trying to keep 12 corks submerged with a small hammer. What should we do? We should ignore the stupid corks and swim to shore. We are not called to dispel the darkness; rather, we are called to turn on the light.

How can a young man keep his way pure? By living according to your word. I seek you with all my heart; do not let me stray from your commands. I have hidden your words in my heart that I might not sin against you (Ps. 119:9-11, *NIV*).

We overcome the father of lies by choosing the truth!

There is a peace of God that surpasses all comprehension and guards our hearts and our minds (noema) in Christ Jesus (see Phil. 4:7).

Finally, brethren, whatever is true, whatever is honorable, whatever is right, whatever is pure, whatever is lovely, whatever is of good repute, if there is any excellence and if anything worthy of praise, let your mind dwell on these things. The things you have learned and received and heard and seen in me, practice these things; and the God of peace shall be with you (Phil. 4:8-9).

We can swim to shore if we are experiencing our freedom in Christ. If we have a lot of unresolved conflicts, however, we are just treading water and will eventually sink. In the epilogue that follows, I will demonstrate how resolving personal and spiritual conflicts leads to freedom. Before we get to that, I'd like to share this closing testimony from a missionary who was sinking fast. This person's story illustrates the freedom that comes through genuine repentance. She was seeing her psychologist, psychiatrist and pastor once a week just to hold her life together. I had the privilege to meet with her one Friday afternoon and take her through the Steps to Freedom in Christ. Two months later, she sent me this letter:

I would like to share an entry I made in my journal Sunday night after our meeting on Friday.

Since Friday afternoon I have felt like a different person. The fits of rage and anger are gone. My spirit is so calm and full of joy . . . I wake up singing praise to God in my heart. That edge of tension and irritation is gone. The Bible has been really exciting, stimulating and more understandable than ever before. There was nothing dramatic that happened during the session on Friday with Neil, yet I know in the deepest part of my being that something has changed. I am no longer bound by accusations, doubts and thoughts of suicide or murder or other harm that came straight from hell into my head. There is serenity in my mind and spirit, clarity of consciousness that is profound.

I'm excited and expectant about my future now. I know that I'll be growing spiritually again, and will be developing in other ways as well. I look forward happily to the discovery of the person God has created and redeemed, as well as the transformation of my marriage. It is so wonderful to have joy after so long a darkness.

It has been over two months since I wrote that, and I'm firmly convinced of the significant benefits of your ministry. I've been in therapy for months, but there is no comparison with the steps I am able to make now. Not only is my spirit more serene, my head is actually clearer. It is easier to make connections and integrate things now. It seems like everything is easier to understand now.[2]

GOING DEEPER

1. How does what we think about ourselves affect who we are?
2. Have you struggled with a spiritual battle in your mind? How has this affected your ability to overcome your addiction(s)?
3. Why is it not enough to simply cast out a demon of lust, homosexuality or alcoholism?
4. How can we tear down mental strongholds?

Notes
1. E-mail written to Neil Anderson at Freedom in Christ Ministries.
2. Letter written to Neil Anderson at Freedom in Christ Ministries.

Epilogue

For 15 years, Freedom in Christ Ministries has been helping people all over the world resolve their personal and spiritual conflicts through genuine repentance and faith in God. The discipleship tool we use is entitled "The Steps to Freedom in Christ." The Steps can be purchased from our office or from any Christian bookstore. Many Christians can work through the process on their own. However, some cannot and need the help of a godly pastor or counselor. To know how to minister the Steps, read Neil's book entitled *Discipleship Counseling* (Regal Books, 2003).

Helping Christians find their freedom in Christ requires a wholistic answer, which takes into account the reality of the spiritual world. We have to submit to God and resist the devil (see Jas. 4:7). It also requires an understanding of and intentional inclusion of Christ and the Holy Spirit in the process. God is the wonderful counselor and the great physician. Only He can bind up the brokenhearted and set the captives free. He is the one who grants "repentance leading to the knowledge of the truth" (2 Tim. 2:25).

Research has been conducted on this discipleship counseling process in several churches in conjunction with our Living Free in Christ conference. The participants were those who requested further assistance after hearing the message—much of which is included in this book—at the conference. They were given one extended counseling session with a trained encourager. They took a pretest before their counseling session and a posttest three months later. The results showed the following:

- 57% improvement in depression
- 54% improvement in anxiety
- 49% improvement in fear
- 55% improvement in anger
- 50% improvement in tormenting thoughts
- 53% improvement in negative habits
- 56% improvement in self-image

We are not sharing these results to establish confidence in our ministry. The reason this process is so effective is *not* because we are wonderful counselors. Actually, trained lay encouragers did all the counseling for the purpose of this research. It was effective because the Lord was the One who set these people free. Christians bond with their loving heavenly Father after they have resolved their personal and spiritual conflicts, and the Holy Spirit bears witness with their spirit that they are children of God. Every testimony you read in this book is a product of this discipleship counseling process. You, too, can find your freedom in Christ through genuine repentance and faith in God. When you do, your Bible will come alive, and you will grow in the grace and knowledge of our Lord and Savior Jesus Christ. May the good Lord grant you that repentance.

The following page can be cut out for your use. On one side is a description of who you are in Christ. The other side is "The Overcomer's Covenant in Christ." They are tools that you can use to remind yourself of who you are in Christ and the victory you have over sin.

For resources and conferences information contact:

Freedom In Christ Ministries
9051 Executive Park Drive, Suite 503
Knoxville, Tennessee 37923
Phone: (865) 342-4000
Fax: (865) 342-4001
E-mail: info@ficm.org
Website: www.ficm.org

Who I Am in Christ

I Am Accepted

John 1:12	I am God's child.
John 15:15	I am Christ's friend.
Romans 5:1	I have been justified.
1 Corinthians 6:17	I am united with the Lord, and I am one spirit with Him.
1 Corinthians 6:19-20	I have been bought with a price. I belong to God.
1 Corinthians 12:27	I am a member of Christ's Body.
Ephesians 1:1	I am a saint.
Ephesians 1:5	I have been adopted as God's child.
Ephesians 2:18	I have direct access to God through the Holy Spirit.
Colossians 1:14	I have been redeemed and forgiven of all my sins.
Colossians 2:10	I am complete in Christ.

I Am Secure

Romans 8:1-2	I am free from condemnation.
Romans 8:28	I am assured that all things work together for good.
Romans 8:31-34	I am free from any condemning charges against me.
Romans 8:35-39	I cannot be separated from the love of God.
2 Corinthians 1:21-22	I have been established, anointed and sealed by God.
Philippians 1:6	I am confident that the good work God has begun in me will be perfected.
Philippians 3:20	I am a citizen of heaven.
Colossians 3:3	I am hidden with Christ in God.
2 Timothy 1:7	I have not been given a spirit of fear but of power, love and a sound mind.
Hebrews 4:16	I can find grace and mercy to help in time of need.
1 John 5:18	I am born of God and the evil one cannot touch me.

I Am Significant

Matthew 5:13-14	I am the salt and light of the earth.
John 15:1,5	I am a branch of the true vine, a channel of His life.
John 15:16	I have been chosen and appointed to bear fruit.
Acts 1:8	I am a personal witness of Christ.
1 Corinthians 3:16	I am God's temple.
2 Corinthians 5:17-21	I am a minister of reconciliation for God.
2 Corinthians 6:1	I am God's coworker (see 1 Corinthians 3:9).
Ephesians 2:6	I am seated with Christ in the heavenly realm.
Ephesians 2:10	I am God's workmanship.
Ephesians 3:12	I may approach God with freedom and confidence.
Philippians 4:13	I can do all things through Christ who strengthens me.

THE OVERCOMER'S COVENANT IN CHRIST

1. I place all my trust and confidence in the Lord, I put no confidence in the flesh, and I declare myself to be dependent upon God.

2. I consciously and deliberately choose to submit to God and resist the devil by denying myself, picking up my cross daily and following Jesus.

3. I choose to humble myself before the mighty hand of God in order that He may exalt me at the proper time.

4. I declare the truth that I am dead to sin, freed from it and alive to God in Christ Jesus, since I have died with Christ and was raised with Him.

5. I gladly embrace the truth that I am now a child of God who is unconditionally loved and accepted. I reject the lie that I have to perform to be accepted, and I reject my fallen and natural identity, which was derived from the world.

6. I declare that sin shall no longer be master over me because I am not under the Law but under grace, and there is no more guilt or condemnation because I am spiritually alive in Christ Jesus.

7. I renounce every unrighteous use of my body, and I commit myself to no longer be conformed to this world but rather to be transformed by the renewing of my mind. I choose to believe the truth and walk in it, regardless of my feelings or circumstances.

8. I commit myself to take every thought captive to the obedience of Christ, and I choose to think upon that which is true, honorable, right, pure and lovely.

9. I commit myself to God's great goal for my life to conform to His image. I know that I will face many trials, but God has given me the victory and I am not a victim but an overcomer in Christ.

10. I choose to adopt the attitude of Christ, which was to do nothing from selfishness or empty conceit, but with humility of mind I will regard others as more important than myself. I will not merely look out for my own personal interests but also the interests of others. I know that it is more blessed to give than to receive.

BOOKS AND RESOURCES BY
DR. NEIL T. ANDERSON

CORE MESSAGE AND MATERIALS

The Bondage Breaker and study guide and audiobook (Harvest House Publishers, 2000)—with well over 1 million copies in print, this book explains spiritual warfare, what our protection is, ways that we are vulnerable and how we can live a liberated life in Christ.

Breaking Through to Spiritual Maturity (Regal Books, 2000)—this curriculum teaches the basic message of Freedom in Christ Ministries.

Discipleship Counseling and videocassettes (Regal Books, 2003)—combines the concepts of discipleship and counseling, and the practical integration of theology and psychology, for helping Christians resolve their personal and spiritual conflicts through repentance.

The Steps to Freedom in Christ and interactive videocassette (Regal Books, 2000)—this discipleship counseling tool helps Christians resolve their personal and spiritual conflicts.

Victory over the Darkness and study guide, audiobook and video-cassettes (Regal Books, 2000)—with well over 1 million copies in print, this core book explains who you are in Christ, how you walk by faith, how your mind and emotions function and how to relate to one another in Christ.

SPECIALIZED BOOKS

The Biblical Guide to Alternative Medicine with Dr. Michael Jacobson (Regal Books, 2003)—develops a grid by which you can evaluate medical practices. It applies the grid to the world's most recognized philosophies of medicine and health.

Blessed Are the Peacemakers with Dr. Charles Mylander (Regal Books, 2002)—explains the ministry of reconciliation and gives practical steps for being reconciled with others.

Breaking the Bondage of Legalism with Rich Miller and Paul Travis (Harvest House Publishers, 2003)—an exposure and explanation of legalism and how to overcome it.

The Christ-Centered Marriage with Dr. Charles Mylander (Regal Books, 1997)—explains God's divine plan for marriage and the steps that couples can take to resolve their difficulties.

Christ-Centered Therapy with Dr. Terry and Julianne Zuehlke (Zondervan Publishing House, 2000)—a textbook explaining the practical integration of theology and psychology for professional counselors.

Daily in Christ with Joanne Anderson (Harvest House Publishers, 2000)—this popular daily devotional is being used by thousands of Internet subscribers every day.

Finding Hope Again with Hal Baumchen (Regal Books, 1999)—explains depression and how to overcome it.

Freedom from Addiction with Mike and Julia Quarles (Regal Books, 1997)—using Mike's testimony, this book explains the nature of chemical addictions and how to overcome them in Christ.

Freedom from Fear with Rich Miller (Harvest House Publishers, 1999)—explains fear, anxiety and disorders, and how to overcome them.

Freedom in Christ Bible (Zondervan Publishing House, 2002)—a one-year discipleship study with notes in the Bible.

Getting Anger Under Control with Rich Miller (Harvest House Publishers, 1999)—explains the basis for anger and how to control it.

God's Power at Work in You with Dr. Robert L. Saucy (Harvest House Publishers, 2001)—a thorough analysis of sanctification and practical instruction on how we grow in Christ.

Leading Teens to Freedom in Christ with Rich Miller (Regal Books, 1997)—this discipleship counseling book focuses on teenagers, their problems and how to solve them.

One Day at a Time with Mike and Julia Quarles (Regal Books, 2000)—this devotional helps those who struggle with addictive behaviors and how to discover the grace of God on a daily basis.

Released from Bondage with Dr. Fernando Garzon and Judith E. King (Thomas Nelson, 2002)—contains personal accounts of bondage with explanatory notes showing how people found their freedom in Christ, and how the message of Freedom in Christ can be applied to therapy with research results.

The Seduction of Our Children with Steve Russo (Harvest House Publishers, 1991)—explains what teenagers are experiencing and how parents can be equipped to help them.

Setting Your Church Free with Dr. Charles Mylander (Regal Books, 1994)—this book on Christian leadership also explains corporate bondage and how it can be resolved in Christ.

The Spiritual Protection of Our Children with Peter and Sue Vander Hook (Regal Books, 1996)—using the Vander Hook's experience, this book explains how parents can help their children.

A Way of Escape with Russ Rummer (Harvest House Publishers, 1998)—explains sexual strongholds and how they can be torn down in Christ.

Who I Am in Christ (Regal Books, 2001)—describes in 36 short chapters who you are in Christ and how He meets your deepest needs.

VICTORY OVER THE DARKNESS SERIES

Overcoming Negative Self-Image with Dave Park (Regal Books, 2003)

Overcoming Addictive Behavior with Mike Quarles (Regal Books, 2003)

Overcoming Depression with Joanne Anderson (Regal Books, 2004)

Overcoming Doubt (Regal Books, 2004)

THE BONDAGE BREAKER SERIES

Finding Freedom in a Sex-Obsessed World (Harvest House Publishers, 2004)

Finding God's Will in Spiritually Deceptive Times (Harvest House Pub-lishers, 2003)

Praying by the Power of the Spirit (Harvest House Publishers, 2003)

YOUTH BOOKS

Awesome God with Rich Miller (Harvest House Publishers, 1996)

The Bondage Breaker—Youth Edition with Dave Park (Harvest House Publishers, 2001)

Extreme Faith with Dave Park (Harvest House Publishers, 1996)

Higher Ground with Dave Park and Dr. Robert L. Saucy (1999)[*]

Purity Under Pressure with Dave Park (Harvest House Publishers, 1995)

Radical Image with Dave Park and Dr. Robert L. Saucy (Harvest House Publishers, 1998)[*]

Real Life with Dave Park (Harvest House Publishers, 2000)[*]

Reality Check with Rich Miller (Harvest House Publishers, 1996)

Righteous Pursuit with Dave Park (Harvest House Publishers, 2000)

Stomping Out Depression with Dave Park (Regal Books, 2001)

Stomping Out Fear with Rich Miller and Dave Park (Harvest House Publishers, 2003)

Stomping Out the Darkness with Dave Park (Regal Books, 1999)

Ultimate Love with Dave Park (Harvest House Publishers, 1996)

[*] Available from Freedom in Christ Ministries only